D1591296

"Jason Byassee's *Introduction to the Desert Fathers* is presented in a spirit of humility that befits the subject. He offers simple yet rich engagements with the *Sayings* that use humor, insight, and life experience to prompt readers to reflect with the same tools. Readers who are looking for a place to begin their interaction with the often paradoxical teachings of the desert fathers would do well to begin here."

—Amy Frykholm, Special Correspondent, *Christian Century*

"Jason Byassee has established himself as the master of explaining complex subjects and helping us understand why they matter. He has done it again with the Desert Fathers."

—James C. Howell, pastor of Myers Park United Methodist Church, Charlotte, North Carolina

❧ *An Introduction to the*
Desert Fathers

Cascade Companions

The Christian theological tradition provides an embarrassment of riches: from scripture to modern scholarship, we are blessed with a vast and complex theological inheritance. And yet this feast of traditional riches is too frequently inaccessible to the general reader.

The Cascade Companions series addresses the challenge by publishing books that combine academic rigor with broad appeal and readability. They aim to introduce nonspecialist readers to that vital storehouse of authors, documents, themes, histories, arguments, and movements that comprise this heritage with brief yet compelling volumes.

❧ *An Introduction to the*
Desert Fathers

JASON BYASSEE

Cascade Books
A division of *Wipf & Stock Publishers*
199 West 8th Avenue, Suite 3 • Eugene OR 97401

AN INTRODUCTION TO THE DESERT FATHERS

ISBN13: 978-1-59752-530-5

Cataloging-in-Publication data:

Byassee, Jason

An introduction to the desert fathers / Jason Byassee.

xii + 118 p.; 20 cm.

ISBN13: 978-1-59752-530-5

1. Desert fathers. 2. Spirituality. 3. Spiritual life—Christianity. I. Title

BV4832.3 .B90 2007

Manufactured in the U.S.A.

For Eric

Table of Contents

Preface

✢ I wrote this little book because I found the *Sayings of the Desert Fathers* delightfully applicable to our present-day efforts to live a more intentional spiritual life in the way of Jesus. Their best "advice" might be their form: if you want to follow Jesus more rigorously, ask for a *word* from one more advanced in holiness.

I've often been the beneficiary of an edifying word from another in the course of writing. First, I'm grateful to Kurt Berends for originally proposing the idea of writing this and my previous book *Reading Augustine* with Cascade. Thanks are due to Jon Stock, Charlie Collier, and all the other good souls at Wipf and Stock for publishing these study guides. The evidence is in: a relationship to an extraordinary church like the Church of the Servant King makes you a better publisher. Thanks also to Jeremy Funk, my copy editor at Cascade, who dealt with me about as gently as some of these abbas! The work is certainly the better for it.

The best dispenser of wisdom in my life is my wife, Jaylynn, United Methodist pastor, mother, and *amma* in the way of Christ's wisdom. Our life together with Jack, Sam, and Will is a rigorous but joyful way to learn discipleship. I'm grateful to my employer, the *Christian Century*, especially to my boss David Heim, for originally giving me a platform from which to write for an ecclesial audience somewhere between the parish and the academy. And I'm grateful to Garrett-Evangelical Theological Seminary, North Park Theological

Seminary, Wheaton College, and Northern Seminary for the chance to learn from students I claim to be "teaching" (actually *being* the abba is a terrifying thought!). Writing this book was an excuse constantly to think of and be grateful to God for my own collection of mentors: Tim Conder, James Howell, and Will Willimon above all. Keep giving me words, abbas!

Mostly, I wish to thank my brother, Eric Byassee, my closest friend. Eric is the real artist in my family. He's a guitar player, singer, and general musician extraordinaire who is right now either booking or playing a gig somewhere between Chapel Hill, Nashville, or Austin. I have no better conversation partner on matters having to do with popular culture, sports, music, or life in general. I can't remember a spiritual doldrum I've inhabited from which he hasn't helped lift me. He may be surprised to know he's played the role of "spiritual father" to me, but he indeed has. I treasure our relationship, and I dedicate this book to him.

Introduction

We all have mental images of the desert, images honed by popular culture. The desert as a wild, uncultivated place where only the strong survive: cacti, various reptiles, the odd cowboy.

That image has a degree of truth in some places. Just as often, we have successfully cultivated the desert. Arizona could never have become the retirement mecca that it is without air conditioning and technological advances in procuring water—the latter with some political controversy. The southern United States generally could not have grown so precipitously in population without similar advances. We like the harsh beauty of the desert, viewed comfortably from an air-conditioned room some sixty degrees cooler than it is outside, with critters kept at bay. Though we may still dress up like cowboys, the reality is not so romantic as the carefully crafted Hollywood image.

In the ancient Christian world, the desert also became a city—but not like Mesa or Tucson. It became a city of those fleeing a church grown soft in collusion with the powerful Roman Empire, trying to live out the risky vision of discipleship glimpsed in the gospels. The description grew up in which these were "white martyrs": those whose martyrdom was not colored with the red of their blood but was a "death" nonetheless—of ascetic denial of comforts, sex, and worldly security. The "desert fathers," as they came to be called, did combat not only with their bodies' wants, but also with demons—demons often represented in terrifying bodily form, as in the famous exploits of St. Anthony. The desert fathers have long occupied a certain pride of place in Christian understanding, such that believers far from the desert and well removed from radical ascetic living champion these peculiar ascetics and, in some sense, made them their own.

All that is a bit romantic and far-fetched. The desert fathers often complained about far more mundane things like mere tedium or listlessness. Further, the romantic image of the previous paragraph suggests that the monks were primarily *against* certain things—the Roman world, their own bodies, the demons, and so on.[1] Their self-understanding would have included not only an antagonistic posture but also, or even primarily, an affirming one: the pursuit of an unbridled life with God, in all its severe intimacy. This pursuit was not so individualistic as it often sounds. The monks did write down their exploits for others to read after all, else we wouldn't have *The Sayings of the Desert Fathers* and other texts. Readers of these works become themselves a certain sort of "community" of those who find the monks worth reading for whatever reason. Further, the "desert became a city" to such a degree that monks often complained about the difficulty of finding the solitude they sought. It also made for opportunities for gracious service to others—as when the Cappadocian fathers turned what was once a desert into a city that provided

1. Recent scholarship has suggested that some of the first monks may merely have been tax evaders! See William Harmless, *Desert Christians: An Introduction to the Literature of Early Monasticism* (Oxford: Oxford University Press, 2004), 10. Before an "anchorite" was a cloistered monk, *anakechorekotes* was a technical term regarding the tax status of those who had fled. It later came to mean "fleeing the world to become a monk."

hospital services and affordable housing—unheard of in the ancient world.[2]

Monastic communities have always avidly read the *Sayings* as guides to their own form of costly discipleship and hospitality. Yet their readership also includes those not personally committed to monastic asceticism, from communities whose traditions do not encourage monasticism as a form of Christian living. Mainline Protestant scholars once denigrated monasticism, as was the Reformers' wont from the beginning. Yet mainline and evangelical Protestants are now turning to this literature to inform their own efforts at discipleship.[3] Why?

One guess is the parallel between the political climate now and in the fourth century. We live in a time in which the church has been extraordinarily pliant in the hands of an imperial political regime that demands absolute allegiance. Christians unhappy with that dark alliance, and uninterested in trying to take over the wheel themselves and steer the church's political commitments in another direction, may find solace in the *Sayings*. Another reason may simply be that anti-Catholic bias among Protestants has waned considerably

2. See Brian Daley, "1998 NAPS Presidential Address, Building a New City: The Cappadocian Fathers and the Rhetoric of Philanthropy," *Journal of Early Christian Studies* 7 (1999) 431–61.

3. That Thomas Merton's *The Seven Storey Mountain* (San Diego: HBJ, 1948) had great resonance among Protestants as well as Merton's fellow Catholics is evidenced by the many monastic vocations he inspired (including that of my grandmother). Kathleen Norris's *The Cloister Walk* (New York: Riverhead, 1996) has had a similarly wide appeal—and this from a Protestant theologian and layperson. For an account of how evangelicals are returning to monastic resources see my article "The New Monastics: Alternative Christian Communities." *Christian Century*, October 18, 2005, 38–47.

in the last few generations. This may be for bad reasons—if we're all consumers of religious feeling, what do our religious differences matter anyway? (We might as well attend to monasticism instead of to our own, say, Lutheranism, as we would decide on McDonalds instead of Hardees). All the same, the chastening of antagonism is something churches should celebrate. For good reason or ill, Christ is preached, and the church is closer to a demonstration of the "oneness" of which he spoke (John 17:21).

My own interest in monasticism is rather quotidian. While studying theology at Duke Divinity School, I imbibed a vision of radical discipleship embodied among Mennonites, especially John Howard Yoder, as transmitted by Stanley Hauerwas. If the church really is distinct from the world, both in its form of life and in its dramatic willingness to share communal goods (like money), where is such a church? As a Methodist learning my church heritage's liturgical underpinnings, I was drawn to Catholic forms of liturgy. Where could one find an ecclesial space marked by liturgy done not just tastefully, but sacramentally—so that the presence of God was as palpable as it was in the liturgy about which the fathers and John Wesley speak?[4]

The answer for me was Mepkin Abbey—a Trappist monastery in Moncks Corner (no kidding!), South Carolina.[5]

4. It is from Geoffrey Wainwright at Duke that I learned to speak of John Wesley as a sort of "evangelical catholic."

5. Monastic life at Mepkin and in most other present-day monasteries reflects the sort of communal living that began with the work of such saints as Benedict and Cassian and flowered in the Middle Ages. The sort of desert monasticism reflected in the *Sayings* was rather different. It features mostly people living as hermits, near enough to one another to offer spiritual advice and challenge and to provide spiritual and material

The monks there knew their liturgy. *The Liturgy of the Hours*[6] is the Catholic monastic worship and wisdom that has been handed on and elaborated through the centuries. They also boasted several trained musicians committed not to showing off but to leading worship. There is nothing more lovely than a plain, unaccompanied guitar helping dozens of monks to chant psalms. The worship in that space was as exquisite as any I could imagine. It made me love the psalms anew, and to want to memorize and chant Scripture and ancient prayers. It made me, in short, a better Protestant (!), if by that we mean someone committed to a love of Scripture and personal piety. A friend took a group of drug-troubled teenagers to another Trappist community once. After Lauds, a service of chanting psalms for an hour at 3:20 a.m., he overheard one student say to another, "Man, that was better than getting high." Worship done right is its own form of intoxication.[7]

The liturgical space is breathtaking. It's a bare room with white walls and wooden ceilings, but those ceilings are stories high, leaving ample space in which light and shadow can play,

sustenance to one another. I reflect on my own experience not to suggest that fourth-century Egypt, medieval France, and present-day Mepkin Abbey are identical—far from it. They are linked, however, as they draw on many of the same forms of scriptural and patristic inspiration (the *Sayings* above all). I also move freely between these forms of life to suggest that living as the desert fathers recommend is, indeed, possible. People are presently doing something very much like it. I hope that churches such as my own United Methodist Church can reimagine new ways to integrate this advice into concrete forms of life. Harmless describes the monastic settlements at Scetis as a "colony of hermits" (175).

6. Available in four volumes as *The Liturgy of the Hours According to the Roman Rite* (New York: Catholic, 1975).

7. I owe this story to Professor Peter Dula of Eastern Mennonite University.

inviting the imagination toward prayer. The altar is a great stone slab in the middle of a circular apse, around which the monks gather for adoration during the Eucharistic liturgy. It looks like something you could sacrifice someone on—a not-inappropriate image for Catholic mass. The baptismal font is a similarly granite colored and massive structure, shaped like a diamond, set to bubble occasionally to remind us aurally of baptism. It needn't do so, as monks and visitors alike are constantly touching it and crossing themselves to remember their baptism and give thanks. The monks face one another in their choir stalls, attentive more to the prayer books in front of them than to the people across the way. Those books are extraordinary—hand-written copies of the Psalter, done by monks from a sister abbey in Massachusetts, lovely in every letter. The silence in the space is beautiful, interrupted as it usually is only by the sound of baptismal water dripping off fingers or monks' robes as they shuffle to their stalls. By contrast the bullfrogs and cicadas of low-country South Carolina roar to life outside, audible easily through the walls.

The liturgy is at times beautiful beyond words. The monks' voices sound at once sad and exultant, as befits the psalms they sing. The Eucharistic liturgy occasionally approaches ballet in its beauty, as priests preside who wear the mass as comfortably as I do an old sweatshirt. My favorite moment is at once Catholic and Pentecostal: when the celebrant raises the host and chalice and says the words of institution, all those present who are ordained lift their hands; it is a glimpse of an undivided, sacramental and Pentecostal form of worship! Even the various prayers about and to Mary, on which Protestants occasionally must swallow hard, eventually wear down opposition by their beauty. One can see, even if fleetingly, how liturgy can suffice in place of worldly ambition, money, sex, and family.

These monks were also not dissimilar to the Anabaptist communities of nonviolence about which Yoder and Hauerwas write.[8] They're committed to nonviolence themselves, as all Catholic vowed priests and religious are. Mepkin's prayers echo this commitment. On August 6 one year (the Feast of the Transfiguration), one brother prayed "for those transfigured this day in 1944 at Hiroshima," in a startling overlay of images— one of angelic peace, one of demonic violence. Perhaps more important, the monks' physical bearing exudes peace and reconciliation. Some are quite literally bowed slightly at the waste at all times, not just from age but from a constant habit of bowing toward Christ and one another in the liturgy. Worship should always mark us so dramatically. My wife, a Methodist preacher, tells of the monks' posture in contrast to that of us visitors. During communion, for example, visitors stand in the circle around the altar as we are accustomed—arms crossed, posture slouched. The monks stand ready to bow, as they have countless times before.

These monks hardly live in the desert.[9] Moncks Corner sits on the Ashley and Cooper Rivers as these two flow toward the harbor town of Charleston. My wife and I left the im-

8. To give just one example, Nancy Klein Maguire describes how the Carthusian monks of England rejected Henry VIII's claim to headship over the church in England and paid for it with their blood. See *An Infinity of Little Hours: Five Young Men and their Trial of Faith in the Western World's Most Austere Monastic Order* (New York: Public Affairs, 2006).

9. For a description of monks who do, see my piece on Christ in the Desert Monastery at http://www.thematthewshouseproject.com/criticism/columns/jbyassee/pilgrimage.htm.

maculate silence of the monastery one afternoon and were feasting on world-class crab cakes that night. Further, the "church" and the "world" are more intertwined in today's monasticism. Mepkin Abbey seeks to serve scholars like me with a recently opened, state-of-the-art library, complete with the now-requisite Internet terminals. One day while there, I went to lunch expecting the normal fare of cheese and bread and was met by stacks of Papa John's Pizza, on which the monks were happily munching.

The monastery has its characters. One, brother Joseph, is the "liturgical guestmaster," as I call him, for he totters over and turns the pages of the library of prayer books, so bewildered guests can find their way. He joined Gethsemani Abbey in Bardstown, Kentucky, in 1944, when he was seventeen and had just graduated from high school. The love of God is quite physically chiseled into his face. Father Aelred, the guitarist whose voice angels envy, reminds me more of an athletic camp counselor than my stereotype of a cloistered monastic. His kind and wise hospitality to outsiders would shame any evangelical. Abbot Francis Kline was a Julliard-trained musician who presided both at organ and at table until his death in 2006 of cancer. His spirit of gentleness pervaded the place, and in truth, still does. Now his replacement as abbot, Brother Stan, will have to spend more time traveling and less worshipping, like any administrator. One hopes that will not dim the childlike blaze in his eyes. A "younger" monk—actually retirement-age (they get as high a proportion of second-career persons as mainline seminaries do these days) spent one career as an Alaskan king crab fisherman, the most dangerous profession in the world according to insurers. He says he won't eat seafood now since he can tell the difference between fish frozen for months and fish right out of the Bering Sea—so good it intoxicates. He then retired with millions to a ranch in Arizona, on which the Hollywood movie *Tombstone* was filmed. He calls that film "the good mustaches against the bad mustaches." Then he retired anew to Mepkin. He says he misses the movies.

I've gone on at length about Mepkin, a place I've only visited half a dozen times, to make clear that living, breathing communities attempt to imitate the form of life described in the *Sayings*. The differences are key, of course. The *Sayings* describe monks who live in much looser community, perhaps near enough to celebrate Eucharist occasionally and share economically, but in individual cells, with far fewer breaks in a rigorous course of solo prayer. Western-style cloistered monasteries originated separately and take their inspiration more from Saint Benedict's *Rule* than from the *Sayings*.[10] Yet, these literatures and their imagined communities bleed into one another, as monks in cloistered community and hermits alike learn from one another's founding documents. The similarities remain striking, however: forswearing the world in a certain sense, taking of difficult vows, devotion to unending streams of prayer. And perhaps most important, this: a witness to the broader church that a life of poverty, chastity, and obedience is extraordinarily beautiful and ought to attract smaller-version imitators among us who do not or cannot go all the way.

10. Benedict, Saint, Abbot of Monte Cassino, *The Rule of St. Benedict*, trans. Anthony C. Meisel and M. L. del Maestro (New York: Image, 1975).

In this study guide on the *Sayings*, I write as one attracted to such a life, committed to imitating it insofar as a married person with children and academic and journalistic reputations to maintain can do so. I write for those interested enough in this oddly ancient, oddly relevant form of living to take up and read. My hope is finally for new and faithful forms of life to spring up in such unexpected places as mainline and evangelical Protestant lives, as befits a Lord who can make streams in the desert.

This Study Guide will follow the same pattern as our previous guide on Augustine's *Confessions*.[11] Hopefully, all participants can use the Penguin edition, *The Desert Fathers: Sayings of the Early Christian Monks*.[12] We expect groups to read along, for it is the ancient Christian texts that provide the nourishment here; this guide is only the seasoning. Or to shift the metaphor, these pages offer spectacles through which to view the texts. In them I will try to clarify what might confuse, and to draw attention to what might otherwise be missed. The questions at the end of each chapter are meant as points of departure for fuller discussion among yourselves about how to perceive God in these ancient texts, and how to live accordingly. A bibliography provides further resources.

11. Jason Byassee, *Reading Augustine: A Guide to the Confessions* (Eugene, OR: Cascade, 2006).

12. Benedicta Ward, trans., *The Desert Fathers: Sayings of the Early Christian Monks*, Penguin Classics (New York: Penguin, 2003).

Questions

1. What's your initial impression with those who take monastic vows? With monasteries? How have those been formed? (experience? popular depiction in art? reading?).

2. Are there other settings, besides anything religious, in which you have experienced God in silence? Or in the keeping of difficult promises?

I. Progress in Perfection

✣ One doesn't have to read long in the *Sayings* to realize that these people were serious! There is a severity to desert spirituality not less intense than that of the weather in Upper Egypt. Christians fled to the desert to avoid the easy alliance between the world and the kingdom. They wished to do as St. Anthony did: to hear the summons of Christ to leave behind family and possessions in order to follow Jesus in costly ways.[1] If the *Sayings* sound harsh to our ears, we must remember that the most "compassionate" thing one serious ascetic can do for another is to remind one of the importance of their mutual calling—to call the other to ongoing repentance and Christlike divestment of themselves.

The oddity of this genre is immediately apparent. What is this work *for*? How was it used in ancient Christianity? There is no clear scholarly consensus on this question, but clearly it was used to encourage others to similar forms of life, whether fellow monks in the desert or those reading in more "worldly" places, like Alexandria, who would pursue a milder sort of asceticism within a more ordinary life in Roman north Africa. As we shall see, visitors from the city would often pursue monks of great reputation for spiritual advice, though with limited success. At least that trope in the *Sayings* suggests the authors' intent was to reach those beyond the desert.

1. Narrated by St. Athanasius in *The Life of Antony, and the Letter to Marcellinus*, trans. Robert C. Gregg, *The Classics of Western Spirituality* (New York: Paulist, 1980).

Even a quick reading reveals that the *Sayings* do not easily fall into separate categories under these chapter headings. "Pursuit in Perfection" could apply to any number of sayings not in this chapter, just as many other sayings could fit well into this one. The work's loose organization is also clear from its breakdown into distinct, easily separable "sayings" that could be repeated in quite different contexts without loss. The *Sayings* work fine as signatures appended to e-mails today because one need not know the broader context of the whole work to read them with profit—as opposed to a quote from, say, Augustine's *Confessions*. And yet, these originally had distinct historical settings-in-life, with particular monks and their stories.[2] As a Christian minister, I can say they seem to me perfectly suited for the task that Catholics think of as "confession." That is, for the spiritual advisor's task of discerning the state of one with whom she is speaking and providing precisely the sort of good word needed at the moment. The *Sayings* suit those who would enact the sort of request often described there: the seeking of a spiritual word from a master by a novice.

We can quickly see both the appealing nature of the *Sayings* and their worrisome dark side in this first chapter. The unappealing first: there seems to be a kind of body-denying ethic at work here, as though it would be easy to be Christian if we were disembodied. The "tongue" and the "belly" are problems to be bridled. We are told to give up "self-will," to embrace "suffering," while a monk who lives "as though buried

---

2. As Harmless points out in great detail in his *Desert Christians*: A particular "word of salvation' was not meant, in the first instance, for everyone. It was a 'word' for *this* monk on *this* occasion, a key specially fitted to unlock a particular heart" (172).

in a tomb" is praised. We are to "avoid the company" of other people, and in the crescendo of the chapter, we are warned not to "make friends with a woman, or a boy, or a heretic." Christianity's nature as an incarnational faith, in which God is not mere spirit but takes on flesh to share our lot, seems to be under threat here. Death is loved, other people are shunned, and anyone who differs (especially women and those judged outside the faith) is cast aside.

And yet the *Sayings* do present a side to themselves that is immediately appealing. For those whose faith is so rigorous that they give up family, progeny, and wealth to pursue it are given surprisingly few demands to meet on the way to salvation. "Wherever you go, keep God in mind; whatever you do, follow the example of holy Scripture; wherever you are, stay there and do not move away in a hurry. If you keep to these guide-lines, you will be saved" (I.1). Really? That's all? Think about God, follow scripture, and don't move around: the first two seem appropriately "religious," the last, not so much. In fact, it is hard to imagine in our highly mobile culture. And yet it is striking that we are not told to memorize the creed, avoid all sin, exercise heroic virtue— just to meditate on God and stay put.

Yet the very next saying seems to suggest salvation by another route altogether: "Do not trust in your own righteousness. Do not go on sorrowing over a deed that is past. Keep your tongue and your belly under control" (I.2). Again, the first two seem sufficiently religious, the last one not so much. Yet we live in an age that shows maniacal obsession with the tongue and the belly, and very little concern over whose

righteousness we trust, or over what deeds we remember.[3]
If anything, our cult of thinness is far more severe than the
desert fathers here. Further, the severity of the desert stands
in contrast to a rather minor plea—to foreswear thought of
one's own righteousness, and not to remember past deeds
with sadness. That's all? The contrast with the previous saying
is striking. For Rowan Williams, the *Sayings'* divergence from
one another is precisely their genius. Such diversity suggests
there is no one monolithic approach to Christian faith, but
rather that the church must wisely direct those in her care in
accordance with their present spiritual state, on the way to
increasing growth.[4] In one instance, one believer may need
this word about the belly; in another, the previous about stay-
ing put. The presumably "irreligious" nature of those claims
is also an important sign for us. "Religion" is a modern con-
cept, if by it we mean a distinct set of feelings and desires that
are private and unrelated to politics or art or friendship. In
the ancient world, "religion" was not so neatly sequestered
from the things that matter in life. Faith more obviously determined where one lived, what one ate. So ought our faith,

3. Sarah Coakley comments on our culture's extraordinary irreligious
asceticism: "In the late twentieth-century affluent West, the 'body,' to be
sure, is sexually affirmed, but also puritanically punished in matters of
diet or exercise; continuously stuffed with consumerist goods, but guiltily
denied particular foods in aid of the 'salvation' of a longer life; taught that
there is nothing *but* it (the 'body'), and yet asked to discipline it with an 'I'
that still refuses complete materialistic reduction" (62). Coakley's complete
article is titled "The Eschatological Body: Gender, Transformation, and
God," *Modern Theology* 16 (2000) 61–73.

4. See Williams's extraordinary treatment of the desert fathers in
Where God Happens: Discovering Christ in One Another (Boston: New
Seeds, 2005).

the desert fathers suggest, affect the nitty-gritty reality of our ordinary lives.[5]

At their worst the monks can seem simply neurotic and world-denying. At their best they live a fulsome Christian life that witnesses to the rest of the church in their time and ours. Section I.6 suggests an emphasis on the monks at their best: "As far as I can tell, abba, I think anyone who controls himself and makes himself content with just what he needs and no more, is indeed a monk."[6] This theme recurs throughout the *Sayings*: simply living in the desert is nothing special; simply living in the world is nothing unholy. One can renounce one's own desires and live fully toward God and others in both places. To say otherwise would tempt a monk to the sin of pride—which was far more worrisome in their day than ours. A later saying suggests this view of "vocation," that is, the search for God's call on our lives: "'Surely all works please God equally? Scripture says, Abraham was hospitable and God was with him; Elijah loved quiet and God was with him; David was humble and God was with him.' So whatever you find you are drawn to in following God's will, do it and let your heart be at peace" (I.11). For those who reject the world and who seek to surpass their fellow Christians in pursuit of radical holiness, this sounds like an extraordinary affirmation of quite ordinary spiritual practice. Our desires, when prop-

5. For a scholarly account of the shifts of meaning for the word *religion* in modernity, see Nicholas Lash, *The Beginning and the End of 'Religion'* (Cambridge: Cambridge University Press, 1996). Or attend to this vignette that Stanley Hauerwas likes to tell about what a Jewish colleague from his days at Notre Dame used to say: any religion that doesn't tell you what to do with your pots and pans and genitals simply cannot be interesting!

6. *The Desert Fathers*, 3–4. We shall use parenthetical citations from here on.

erly ordered, are good and God-given and lead us naturally to doing that which God calls us to do. Of course, ironing out our desires so they reach toward God may be a more difficult task than this presentation suggests.

These *Sayings* can help with that task however. Note how many of these restrictions and commendations are strongly *communal* in nature. What we eat, what we want, whether we are hospitable, the sort of quiet we seek—all these have profoundly to do with how we interact with others. Williams sees the heart of the *Sayings* as the effort to become Christ to the other—that is, to point one's sister or brother toward God and others in every moment.[7] This is both a difficult task and a high calling, the attainment of which would indeed be "perfection." The great abba Pambo said as much at the moment of his death: "I go to the Lord as one who has not yet made a beginning in the service of God" (I.16).

Questions

1. What has your experience of the desert been, whether in actually visiting or in imagining it?

2. Many of these *Sayings* take the form of a younger monk approaching an older and wiser one for an edifying word. To whom do you go for such wisdom? Can we approach the *Sayings* literature itself that way? As though it might present us with a saving "word"?

---

7. Williams, *Where God Happens*, 24, describes the goal of desert asceticism this way: "Insofar as you open such doors for another, you gain God, in the sense that you become a place where God happens for somebody else."

3. Do these first few sayings suggest rejection of oneself, others, and the world—or acceptance? Or some middle ground between?

4. How do these *Sayings* envision the Christian life? How does that compare with your own experience of Christianity?

II. Quiet

❧ It is hard to find quiet in our world. Cell phones ring and people talk loudly in places they never used to. We fret if we haven't received an e-mail in the last few minutes, as though worried we shall cease to exist. Blackberry, appropriately nick-named "crackberry," keeps us linked to the Internet like sick people to an IV. David Brooks describes the moment when the airline asks passengers to turn off their cell phones as no more welcome than a request to rip out their tracheas would be.[1]

Even when we try for quiet, when we act on our vague sense that it would be a good thing, we are not innately good at it. In my time at the monastery, I find I enjoy the startling quiet for a few minutes, and quickly become antsy and bored. Or else I fall asleep (having been up since 3 a.m. for morn-ing vigils, after all)! So I venture off in pursuit of some task: something to read from the monastic library, a monk to talk to, studying that I have brought with me. This initial objec-tion to quiet must be overcome and the quiet restored. That process of resistance and overcoming must be repeated until the quiet is, once again, "natural." Only then can we begin to listen for God.

Or so spiritual writers from the Christian tradition throughout time have held. This section contains sayings that show us why. Although we have more material here to

1. David Brooks, *On Paradise Drive: How We Live Now (And Always Have) in the Future Tense* (New York: Simon & Schuster, 2004) 235.

21

which to object—such as disparagement of women at II.7 and II.13—we also have lovely, if puzzling, appeals to the importance of quiet for the spiritual life. Antony[2], the patron saint of the desert, insists that as "Fish die if they stay on dry land," so the monk cannot survive outside his cell (II.1). Abba Moses says, in his typically cryptic and wise way, "Go and sit in your cell, and your cell will teach you everything" (II.9). Clearly the goal is not to pay attention to the inside of the cell, as we often do when bored—counting ceiling tiles or attending to the rustic surroundings. Abba Arsenius criticizes brothers who tell him that the rustling noise is the shaking of the reeds. For "If a man sits in silence and hears the voice of a bird, he does not have quiet in his heart; how much more difficult is it for you, who hear the sound of these reeds?" (II.5). In contemporary spirituality, we are often encouraged to notice the handiwork of God in creation; here, precisely the opposite advice is given. A lovely sound is a distraction that the good monk will not even notice.

Stories with archbishops in the *Sayings* normally turn out in similar ways to the two here: with the monk in question fleeing, and the archbishop rejected. This is more startling in an ancient context, in which the bishop must be treated with the same respect due to Christ himself. (In our day, disrespecting an ecclesial figure is more to be expected than not!) The wariness about ecclesial dignitaries suggests the monks' discomfort with the ruling version of Christianity in their day, with its penchant for gaudy displays of wealth and quick obedience to imperial power. Nevertheless, even

2. His name is sometimes rendered in English as "Anthony," at other times, as in this edition, as "Antony."

an archbishop in Alexandria—one of the five holiest sees in ancient Christianity since legend held the apostle Mark had evangelized the place personally—is interested in the monks and eager for their support. This is partly for political reasons. Monks in ancient Christianity occasionally acted rather more like mafia figures than the monks at Mepkin Abbey—beating up opponents, breaking up rival meetings, furthering or hindering the political agendas of the bishops they supported or opposed. The memory of Sts. Athanasius and Cyril, both of Alexandria, is somewhat tainted by the enlisting of such monastic muscle.

Yet in the *Sayings* the monks see bishops as threats for a different reason and are eager to distance themselves from them and all they represent. Here Abba Arsenius cleverly elicits a promise from the archbishop to do whatever he, the wise guide, asks. In appropriate fashion for a spiritual seeker or novice, the archbishop agrees. "Wherever you hear Arsenius is, do not go there," he insists (II.4). Later, in the same saying, we get an explanation: "If I have opened the door to you, I must open it to all, and then I shall no longer be able to live here." Later, a wealthy woman from Rome is sent by Archbishop Theophilus to Arsenius. He rejects her, rather harshly. He fears that her gossip about him upon her return from her pious tour will "turn the sea into a highway with women coming to see me." This is worrisome not only for its destruction of his quiet, but because "the enemy uses women to attack holy men," as Theophilus explains to a distraught and stricken pilgrim (II.7). This description betrays the ancient prejudice, contrary to our own, that women were somehow innately more sexually inclined than men, and so impossible to resist if inclined to make sexual advance, which they undoubtedly would. It also suggests that monks wanted to be left in peace, to have no visitors at all, especially not bishops or women. Why?

We see a hint in the final saying in this section: "There were three friends, serious men, who became monks." Two do praiseworthy things commended by Christ himself in Scripture: one becomes a peacemaker, another a visitor of the sick. The third chooses the quiet of solitude. When they meet to consider their lives, the first two are weary and troubled. The third has a parable. He pours water, which only after a moment is still, allowing them to see their faces in its surface. "So it is with anyone who lives in a crowd; because of the turbulence, he does not see his sins: but when he has been quiet, above all in solitude, then he recognizes his own faults." Quiet is a kind of laboratory of the spirit, in which all other variables have to be controlled—friendship, visits by strangers, even the hint of sexual attraction, desire for fame, sheer busyness. Only when the painstaking work of achieving quiet is accomplished—once the surface of our spirit is calm—can we begin to see our sins, root them from our spirits, and leave space for holiness to bloom.

Questions

1. Have you ever sought, or perhaps even achieved, the sort of quiet about which the *Sayings* speak here?

2. Does the misogyny of these texts make them totally un-readable, or can we filter that out and still profit from reading?

3. How do you "talk" about quiet? How does the portrait of Arsenius and others shunning fame square with the writing and widespread distribution of stories such as these?

4. In our day, hermits are rarely "famous." Celebrities are (though a recent "reality TV" show about the Monastery of Christ in the Desert may yield the odd hybrid creature of the "celebrity monk" . . .). Most of us would like to be well known and well spoken of by others. What would the shunning of fame (that is, the pursuit of ignorance of our exploits by others) mean for us?

III. Compunction

✣ The air of death hangs rather heavily over this section. The comments here in favor of grieving, an almost eager anticipation of the grave, in derision of laughter and even of life itself, suggest a denial of creation itself in the *Sayings*, a denial not unlike that of ancient gnostics who held that this material world is created by some inferior and reckless god. We are to meditate "like the criminals in prison" (III,2). We must "remember the souls in hell" (III.3). Abraham is commended for having "built himself a grave" when he entered the promised land—a detail perhaps accidentally left out of the biblical narrative itself! (III.13). An inconsolable widow is held up as an example for watching monks (III.11). In this case, we should recognize that this is not just a romantic image in a modern sense, as when we cry over a lost lover. It is rather a loss of livelihood and protection—almost a loss of life really, to lose a husband in that world. And mostly we're told to mourn, like the houses in which children were struck down in Egypt, for our God is "a consuming fire" (III.16, 24 & 25).[1]

1. Douglas Burton-Christie has written about the desert fathers' sophisticated approach to the Bible. Only occasionally do they quote it directly, as with the quote from Hebrews 12:29 about God as a "consuming fire" at III.16. More often Scripture is alluded to, built upon, referenced typologically to build up a scriptural imagination, as in the reference to the widow at III.11 (see Luke 21:1–4 and parallels). See his *The Word in the Desert: Scripture and the Quest for Holiness in Early Christian Monasticism*. (New York: Oxford University Press, 1993).

At this point it is important to remember that the flight of serious Christians into the Egyptian desert did not begin as a sociopolitical "statement" over against a church overly compliant to the empire, appealing though that picture is. It was not intentionally an effort to turn the desert into a city, an oasis of spiritual care on behalf of the poor and destitute, though it may have become that. It was, at first, an effort to "flee from the wrath," as Jesus himself counseled in his first recorded sermon in Mark's gospel (Mark 1:15–16). It was an effort to seek salvation, in imitation of John the Baptist's flight to deserted places, and in imitation of Jesus' wrestling with temptations in the desert. Both of those, of course, are echoes of Israel's wandering in the wilderness for forty years. This is not to say the effort was for "individual" salvation—no one in the ancient world thought of him- or herself as a distinct unit of consciousness, easily severed from others without difficulty—we have modern times to thank for that notion.[2] It was, rather, an effort to heed the costly call of Jesus to forsake all else and follow, to struggle against demons and the forces of evil, to be those to "weep now" in anticipation of an eschatological future of laughter (Matt 5:4, Mark 8:34). It was a search for salvation—of a different sort than we imagine in our churches for the most part, but salvation nonetheless. In one of these sayings, Macarius the Great is summoned to preach to an eager gathering (a revival meeting of sorts!). When those who anticipate a profound word from

2. For more on this see Michael Hanby's *Augustine and Modernity* (London: Routledge, 2003). He writes about Augustine, since the modern notion of the self has often been blamed on Augustine. Hanby actually sees Augustine as the way out of any such individualistic notion of personhood.

the famous sage turn to hear him, he weeps: "Let us pray and weep, my brothers, before we go hence to the place where our tears consume our bodies" (III.9). They all weep—and ask his prayers. Quite an altar call.

Even so, there are moments in this chapter that weigh against some of our stereotypical portraits of monastic living. The great Macarius of Egypt is asked why his body remains the same whether he eats well or fasts: "A wooden poker which turns over and over the brushwood in the fire is itself being slowly burnt away. So if a man cleanses his mind in the fear of God, the fear of God also consumes his body" (III.8). There is here no easy division between an inner, spiritual self that is good, and an outer, physical self that is bad. Macarius's manner of prayer and anticipation of judgment makes for a quite physical repercussion on his body. There is also here no sense of spiritual superiority on the part of the monks. Silvanus reports back from an experience of rapture that he "saw many of our kind going down to torment, and many from the world going into the kingdom" (III.15). A clear biblical theme is sounded here: those who think themselves holy are in trouble; those not so inclined to pride, less "religious" though they may be, are far better off (see Luke 18:9–14). Even the description above of Macarius's tearful revival sermon cuts against our notion of individual spiritual heroes. He is summoned to preach, and instead leads the whole assembly in weeping together and in seeking prayers. We, in turn, read this saying and are encouraged to respond similarly. Community is created. Perhaps a bit of a soggy one, but community nonetheless.

It remains a potent spiritual tradition in the Greek-speaking Christian east that tears are a kind of second baptism. Baptism itself washes away original sin and sins already committed. After that, western Christians generally speak of confession and absolution as the recourse for postbaptismal sin. Eastern spiritual advice focuses on tears, "compunction": that is, sorrow for sin and a quite physical and emotional penance and resolve to "sin no more." Perhaps our inability to comprehend such forms of devotion stems from a loss of fear of divine judgment, so pronounced in the ancient Christian world, and so muted in our efforts to depict God as nice, and Christianity as accessible to all comers.[3] Ammon can say that salvation itself consists in being like criminals in prison, awaiting a ruthless judge, because he has a notion of a coming judgment seat of Christ—one deeply steeped in Christian Scripture (Matt 25:31–46). A tradition of divine judgment appears throughout Scripture and is not muted in Jesus' preaching or in the rest of the New Testament. If anything, it is more pronounced there than anywhere. Find me a notion of hell in the Old Testament and then you can have your facile division between a fire and brimstone Old Testament God and a nice Jesus.

Tears are about the displacement of any struggle for status acquisition before our ultimate Judge. For such posturing marks most of our lives: the effort to succeed, to appear cool and collected, to impress others and do well for ourselves. Tears are the recourse of those who claim no such cool togetherness, of those who have lost loved ones or dreams or public

3. As Hauerwas likes to say, Methodists' lone dogma is that God is nice, and we should be nice too. David Steinmetz, church historian at Duke, likes to summarize Methodist politics this way: "if it moves, affirm it."

face. Naturally, tears can be a way of reerecting emotional boundaries, of saving face, as when someone uses them to avoid responsibility or accusation. But more often, tears are a mess. They acknowledge something is profoundly wrong, and we have no easy recourse to right them.

This is why tears are so prominently called for in Jesus' famous preaching in the Sermon on the Mount. Those who weep now know this entire cosmos is out of sorts. Even with Jesus' inbreaking kingdom and the Spirit's gradual work for redemption among us, this world is not yet the kingdom. Sin still reigns in more places than not. The kingdoms of this world have not yet become the kingdoms of our Lord and of his Christ, as Revelation 11:15 promises they one day will. Those with the gift of tears recognize this. Those who turn to a Pollyanna form of Christianity that pretends to the present goodness of everything simply delude themselves and others.[4] Those who weep acknowledge the way things genuinely are, and their inability to prevail on God or anyone else to make them right. Those who weep also rightly acknowledge our willful complicity in sin—a poignant word for Christians in a North America filled with obese people, spending tens of billions of dollars a year on diet products, while the rest of the world starves: "Some brothers were eating together at a love-feast, one of the brothers at the table laughed. When John saw it, he wept, and said, 'What do you think that this brother has in his heart, that he could laugh when he ought to weep because he is *dining on charity*'" (III.6).

4. A friend of mine takes umbrage with Oprah's pastoral statement to America during her pseudoworship service in Yankee Stadium after 9/11. She claimed, "Every time you lose a loved one, you gain a star in the sky." His appropriate reply: "No you don't."

Tears may not only be a tonic for what ails our age of happy and chatty Christians. It may also be a way to respond to conflict in the church or elsewhere. As a former pastor, I can attest to the way that ecclesial problems can eat at those called to oversee congregations. One word of criticism, one whiff of disenchantment from those in the ranks of my church, and I was psychologically shot for days. This may have been due to a pastoral immaturity—a sense that conflict is bad, and praise of the pastor all-important. In contrast, remember the hermit's comparison of the search for tears (a difficult one in the seeker's case) and Israel's forty-year wandering: "Tears are the promised land. When you reach them you will no longer be afraid of the conflict" (III,27). Tears, perhaps rightly, name the fact that I am already wretched, that things are out of sorts, and we should have no pretension to their easy resolution. Having recognized this, we see that conflict with others no longer seems to be something to be eschewed for its own sake. It's not surprising that we, church members, will argue and fail to understand one another, in this age that is passing away. Therefore, perhaps counter-intuitively, tears are a first step toward repaired relationship in the church. For with them we can be honest about our differences, no longer blame the other for causing problems (for they are ever with us), and set about caring well for a fellow creature who is, with me, entangled in sin, and who is likewise stretching out toward redemption . . . with tears.

Questions

1. What relationship, if any, exists between the tears here called for and the emotional release we feel after a good cry?

2. Have tears been a constituent part of your Christianity? Should they be?

3. Do we have here the desert fathers at their most morose, or can we argue for the presentation of compunction here as capturing something essential we often miss?

IV. Self-Control

 In this section, we see the desert fathers at both their least and most appealing. When a monk will not even touch his mother's body, since "a woman's body is fire. Simply because I was touching you, the memory of other women might come into my mind" (IV.68). Again, the idea of woman as temptress, never fully shrugged off by the church, is painfully obvious. Elsewhere, a mother begs to see her sons in the desert, insisting "Am I not your mother? Have I not given you milk at the breast, and now every hair of my head is grey?" The great Abba Poemen insists to her that the way to see them in the next life is *not* to see them now. She goes away happy! (IV.33). Yet we modern readers are unconvinced. Surely an overly facile distinction between misery in this world and happiness in the next is one of the most dangerous hallmarks of Christianity, able to justify any amount of cruelty and suffering now for the sake of pie in the sky later.

Even in these two stories, wretched though they are in some respects, there is something to be commended. Both involve a monk's mother. So both call to mind the biblical theme of renunciation of biological family in return for the new family of the church (Mark 3:21; 3:31–35; Luke 12:49–53). The contrast between the two may be overdrawn—whatever conflict Jesus first has with his biological mother, she clearly has pride of place in the new family of the church by the end of the story (John 19:26–27; Acts 1:14). Nevertheless, the picture is clear and perhaps salutary for us: the church requires a break with what came before, and a radical embrace of what's new.[1] The egregious nature of the contrast is perhaps intentional. As Flannery O'Connor famously said about her own use of the grotesque in fiction, "to the hard of hearing you shout, and for the almost-blind you draw large and startling figures."[2]

Even as we see something commendable in these troublesome sayings, others seem simply dubious. Zeno is hungry for a cucumber. To remind himself that such theft would carry a heavy penalty, he exposes himself to sun for five days, without water. "His thoughts, as it were, spoke to him saying, 'We can't bear such torment.' So he said to himself, 'If you can't bear torment, do not steal in order to eat'" (IV.17). This seems like the sort of cruelty to one's body for the sake of a rather pious lesson of the soul for which the church has rightly long been criticized. Not all we find here is salutary in the way its authors intended. Perhaps it can be an occasion *not* to "go and do likewise"!

We also see the desert fathers at their most obviously appealing in this chapter. Even a hint of humor starts to creep into their stories, perhaps despite themselves. We see it especially with regard to sayings about mindfulness, awareness of

1. For further suggestions about the conflict between biological and ecclesial families, see Stanley Hauerwas, "Hating Mothers as the Way to Peace," in *Unleashing the Scriptures: Freeing the Bible from Captivity to America* (Nashville: Abingdon, 1993) 117–25; or Will Willimon, "The New Family," in *Peculiar Speech: Preaching to the Baptized* (Grand Rapids: Eerdmans, 1992) 116–22.

2. Flannery O'Connor, *Mystery and Manners*, ed. Robert and Sally Fitzgerald (New York: Farrar, 1957) 34. It seems to me the desert fathers and O'Connor's short stories are very similar sorts of literature: shocking, grotesque, aimed at conversion, and profoundly funny.

the body, and eating. "Often his disciple used to say, 'Come, abba, let us eat.' He would say, 'Haven't we already eaten, my son?' The disciple would reply, 'No, abba.' The hermit used to say, 'If we have not eaten yet, bring the food, let us eat'" (IV.38). A priest from the community at Scetis reported back to his brothers that he saw no one on a visit to Alexandria except the archbishop. They're worried. Was everyone killed? The city razed? "He cheered them by saying, 'I wrestled with my soul not to look at anyone's face except the bishop'" (IV.55). In another story, again about forgetting the rule to flee from women and bishops, a group of brothers dines with the archbishop. They eat what is put before them, saying nothing. Then the archbishop mentions it is veal and picks out an especially appetizing piece for one of the abbas. The brothers stop eating. They're vegetarians. They hadn't noticed they were eating meat, but having been told as much, they will eat no more (IV.63). One hermit visiting another becomes so engrossed in reciting psalms and reading the prophets that the offered lentils go uneaten all night (IV.57). In another case, a monk is proud to avoid the company of women. The abbess chides him: "If you had been a true monk, you would not have looked to see that we are women" (IV.62).

What's going on here? The theme is something like the disciplining of one's habits of attention. Most of us are acutely aware of our need for food and for the affection of the people around us. If we're honest, those things demand extraordinary amounts of our time and attention.[3] For the desert fathers, however, that very time and attention spent feeding ourselves

3. I'm especially aware of this while traveling. When you have to think of what to do for every meal three times a day, you remember that we are indeed embodied creatures.

well and surrounding ourselves with preferred sorts of company are precisely what ought to be occupied with prayer and attention to God. The sort of physical traffic through our mouths and stomach can serve as a distraction, or can even substitute for the traffic through our minds and souls of conversation with God. The desire for pleasing company can easily take the place of the desire for companionship with God's saints both living and dead, whose writings and prayers ought to be echoed in our own. Yet, notice that the desert fathers don't simply say this in as many words. It would be boring to do so! They rather say it with stories that catch us off guard, even as we anticipate them. Not to notice people in so large a city as Alexandria? Not to notice scrumptious veal going into one's mouth until one is told these aren't plain lentils? These sayings, to borrow Emily Dickisnon's words: "tell all the truth, but tell it slant."

At the most basic level, these sayings commend certain fasts. We should abstain from any but the most necessary food and sleep (IV.3–4). Agatho, one of the most beloved of the desert fathers, keeps a stone in his mouth for years to teach himself silence (IV.7). It is hard to put one's foot where a stone already resides! Achillas worries an interlocutor with the blood dripping from his mouth. Yet it is not an injury; it is an answered prayer. He nursed a grievance and asked God for its removal, and "the word turned to blood in my mouth" (IV.9). We are also to abstain from acquisitiveness, even of the most basic "necessities" (Indeed, reading these *Sayings* can help us redefine what is a "necessity"!). Benjamin wants to give a hermit a gift of oil but is told that the same gift he had given years ago is still where he had left it (IV.12). For two decades, Helladius does not even look at his cell's roof (IV.16). The refusal to eat, drink, sleep, speak, or look around sharpens the senses to attend to God as food, drink, interlocutor, source of vision, and beauty. The contrast between the two is intentional, for other things indeed rival our desire for God in all these areas. The desert is a place to wrestle with our desire and seek its fulfillment in its proper place. We all know the hurt a misplaced word can cause. We may be less personally acclimated to the harm eating and drinking and looking can do. A trivial example may help: Henri Nouwen used to remark that when he traveled, he ate too much, drank too much, and looked around too much. Erasure of our lives' normal strictures can cause us to behave in ways we would not otherwise, and this is precisely the reason many *do* travel! Perhaps in contrast, sinking roots in the desert is a way to see these desires for the distraction from God that they indeed are, and to be retrained accordingly.

Even after this word on behalf of asceticism, we can notice a more naturally appealing part of this section's portrait—its gentleness and grace. Even fasting, abstaining, is not an end in itself, for "fasting dries up the channels down which worldly pleasures flow" (IV.47). Fasting is seen as a way of gaining power over our archetypal desire, control of which enables our control over other desires. Even the appeal to silence is clearly not simply a mandate never to talk. For the demons love it when a monk refuses to tell his confessor his sins! (IV.25). Silence is a kind of discernment about speech, an insistence upon giving air to would-be and actual sins, and refusal to chat as a distraction or opportunity for self-inflation.

Even more strikingly, bodily discipline and asceticism take a backseat here to hospitality. As the *Sayings* repeatedly attest, one must give up a fast if an opportunity for hospitality arises (IV.40). Great as fasting is (and the *Sayings* consistently insist on its greatness), it is nothing compared to a refusal to let the sun set on one's anger (IV.15). A heroic fast can lead to illness, but a good meal made by a caring brother can restore health—despite the frequent penchant for total denial of the body (IV.66). In an extraordinary incident involving eating, a brother is tempted to sadden his fellow who coughs on him: "So to tame himself and restrain his own angry thought he picked up what had been spat and put it in his mouth and swallowed it. Then he began to say to himself, 'If you say to your brother what will sadden him, you will have to eat what nauseates you'" (IV.70). The story makes clear that our tastes have to change! Our natural revulsion for phlegm must give way to the point where harming another in the community is what truly sickens us. Having our way with a cutting comment at another's expense is an inclination that must be weakened by fasting, and destroyed. Notice the extraordinary accent on grace, even with the exaggerated figure: it is the other who matters, and our own self-vindicating importance that must be slain.

Questions

1) Is it precisely the gross figures and exaggerated models that make the desert fathers so compelling? Why or why not?

2) What consequences might arise from reading about the goodness of fasting in an age when our culture's vision of beauty leads so directly to people, especially women, punishing their bodies? Can proper feasing and fasting be a resource against such a view?

3) Which is most difficult to discipline: our eating, sleeping, looking, or speaking? Why?

4) Does the reading of these *Sayings*, and discussing them together, itself help *create* a community in which achievement of these sorts of ascetic feats seems more plausible?

V. Lust

⌘ A great gift of the *Sayings* is its oscillation between strenuous rigor and boundless grace. In our own political climate, it is the "conservatives" who are in favor of strict application of difficult rules whatever the public perception, and "liberals" who are for generosity, looser binding by rules, and gracious affirmation of those left out. The distinction is a false one, as the desert fathers show. For here *only* those with a rigorous form of disciplined common life can apply their rules with grace, and only those who are generous about the failings of others can keep at a form of life that's far from easy.

The rule-bound side of the fathers' life together is seen most clearly in what may be the most troubling saying of all. A monk hears that the woman for whom he lusted has died. At night he goes, digs up her corpse, and wipes her blood on his cloak, which he then keeps handy in his cell. "When it smelt too bad, he put it in front of him and said to his temptation, 'Look, this is what you desire. You have it now, be content.' So he punished himself with the smell until his passions died down" (V.22). That *would* do the trick! Even this story, macabre as it is, has a point: lust constricts our world, winnowing our attention down to a particular person with whom we would have our way. It doesn't just objectify the other, though it does that; it objectifies also *the one who lusts*—by enslaving to a certain imagined end, whether realized or not. The monk here shows that the one who's captured his desire and attention is a mere human, doomed to rot like the rest of us. His senses had forgotten this and needed reminding. All the same, a monk who cannot be trusted around a graveyard is probably not the one from whom to take spiritual advice!

Yet we also see here the extraordinarily gentle touch of the desert fathers. The story is told of two brothers who went into town and went their separate ways. One fell into fornication, the other did not. Yet the one who did nothing wrong claimed he had also: "The same thing happened to me . . . Let us go together, and do penance with all our might, and God will pardon us sinners" (V.27). Knowing what we do about the severity of life among the monks, we know this penance cannot have been light. Yet the non-offending (even lying?[1]) monk "did penance not for himself, but for the other, as though he himself had sinned." The secret does not stay with him, however. God reveals to an elder that the fornicator is forgiven "because of the charity of the brother who had not sinned. Truly, this was to lay down his soul for his brother" (John 15:13). Notice, God absolves because of the friend's penance, rather than the offender's.

Did the brother lie to win his brother? In a sense, yes; he had not fornicated. But in a larger sense, no; he told the truth. The two monks are connected to one another—not only as fellow ascetics but as brothers in Christ, relatives in our common ancestor, Adam. The sin of the one is, in a way, the sin of the other. It is not inappropriate to do penance for the sin of another, especially with the goal of winning that one, of helping him, of pushing him to procure forgiveness. Notice how

1. Paul Griffiths describes Augustine's quite strenuous proscription of lying for Christians, one perhaps at odds with the desert fathers, in his *Lying: An Augustinian Theology of Duplicity* (Grand Rapids: Brazos, 2004).

much the brother risks with his fib about fornicating and his faux-confession to sexual sin—he risks loss of his soul even, expulsion from the community if unable to bear the heavy penance. Yet he embraces it, risking even the very soul which he had gone to the desert to save.

We see here an extraordinarily *communal* ethic, one for which the other is genuinely another self, in which the gaining of one's own soul is not more important than the winning of another. St. Paul describes love as that which is poured into our hearts by the very Holy Spirit of God (Romans 5:5). Such love binds us in community and enables us to lay down our lives for our friends. This story of penance is then a vision of the church itself.

These two stories, of the macabre and the charitable, rest rather uneasily alongside one another. Yet that is their genius. This is not a continuous narrative in which one subplot can spoil another with a glaring contradiction. It is rather a piece-meal set of stories, each preserved for its ability to instruct, delight, and move those reading. Perhaps more primordially, the entire *Sayings* collection was designed to help a spiritual director, an abba, to counsel one younger in the faith who was struggling with so common a demon as lust. The stories then serve as a palette does for a painter, presenting all available colors to be used at that one's expert discretion. The abba can produce just the right story for the ailment of the one in front of him: if excessive lust, the macabre and putrid story; if individualism and pride, the one about the two friends. The presence of both colors on the same palette alerts us that rigor and grace are each impossible without the other, and that it takes an extraordinary amount of practical wisdom to know when to apply each.

In this exchange between monks—between abba and seeker or between fornicator and friend—we see the life of the church enacted. The church is the very dwelling place of the Spirit, not less than the Temple in Hebrew Scripture, or the Son of God incarnate in the gospels. As another hermit says, "It is not possible for a man to be recalled from his purpose by harshness and severity; demon cannot drive out demon. You will bring him back to you better by kindness. That is how God acts for our good, and draws us to himself" (IV.28). The sort of wise and rigorous gentleness imaged here is not just pragmatic skill at keeping a diffuse community united (though that's important), it is a glimpse of the way God deals with us, wayward and lost as we are, with sage severity and wise kindness. Two things that seem contradictory are here shown to be inseparable and bordering on indistinguishable.

A young brother confesses his lust to an older one, a hermit. The *Sayings* are unequivocal that lust and other temptations remain, for the holiest of us still has passions within, and, in fact, the absence of struggle means the absence of hope (V.5). Yet the hermit who is sought for advice knows nothing of this, and so scandalizes the young brother by putting him down. While "on the way back to the world" (synonymous for the desert fathers with leaving Christian faith), the brother who has been scandalized and so is leaving bumps into Apollo, who prods him to say what happened. Apollo responds, "Do not be cast down, nor despair of yourself. Even at my age and with my experience of the spiritual life, I am still troubled by thoughts like yours." In William Harmless's telling of a similar story, the confessor asks tenderly, "Am I not a man?"[2] The younger brother agrees to stay. Apollo then dishes out some justice to the hermit, praying to God that the demon striking the younger one would prey on the accuser. The hermit in question cannot stand a minute of the temptation and stumbles out of his cell, back to the world. He gets an earful: he should have offered consolation, he should have imitated God's refusal to break a bruised reed (Matt 12:20), he should emulate God's willingness to preserve us in our weakness. Then Apollo leaves off the "shoulds" and talks, almost ecstatically, about God: "For he makes a man to grieve, and then lifts him up to salvation; he strikes, and his hand heals; he humbles and exalts; he gives death and then life; he leads to hell and brings back from hell." In other words, we are no better than another who faces greater temptation and falls: who's to say how we would fare under similar circumstances? It is only ours to offer consolation, in imitation of the gentleness of Christ, to encourage another back to his cell.

Perhaps surprisingly, the accent in these sayings is against excessive penance. "We cannot make temptations vanish, but

---

2. There are several different versions of the *Sayings* from the ancient world. The one we have been using is organized "systematically," as it is normally described, or according to topic. The other is organized alphabetically according to the name of the abba involved. This particular story comes from an appendix often attached to the alphabetical version for stories involving nameless abbas. Harmless takes it from Columba Stewart's "Radical Honesty about the Self: The Practice of the Desert Fathers," *Sobornost* 12 (1990) 27. The alphabetical version, containing many of the same sayings here but some different ones, is available as *The Sayings of the Desert Fathers: An Alphabetical Collection*, trans. Benedicta Ward (Kalamazoo, MI: Cistercian, 1975). Another related volume is *The Lives of the Desert Fathers: The Historia monachorum in Aegypto*, trans. Norman Russell (Kalamazoo, MI: Cistercian, 1981).

we can struggle against them," we're told (V.16). One can imagine the lethargy in the desert: monks praised elsewhere for not looking at the ceiling for decades but having all that time to think of past sexual experience or inexperience—time dedicated to God but given over to lust—and to the resultant guilt. Yet here the stress is on mercy, not punishment. The very cosmos demands it. A deacon lies with an official's wife and asks a hermit to hide him, so he can do penance. Not long after, the Nile fails to flood (economic disaster for a region whose agriculture was dependent on the annual floodwater that kept the soil fertile). "When they were all saying litanies, it was revealed to one of those holy men that unless the deacon who had hidden with such and such a monk, should return, the water would not rise" (V.26). Mercy keeps the earth spinning on its axis. Without it, nature itself may revolt, bringing disaster on us all: a message our own age could stand to hear.

This section contains innumerable other lessons small and large. One boy, raised in the desert, does not know the sight of women. He is satisfied to learn that they are "monks of the world . . . They wear one kind of dress, and monks of the desert another." The story had to draw a laugh, but it contains a profound teaching: habits of attention that feel ingrained ("natural" to us), such as lust, can be unlearned, substituted with healthy habits of attention. This is akin to my teaching my children to pray before they can object, to pay attention in church as readily as they do to the television. It is hardly obvious that it is easier or more "entertaining" to watch TV than to attend to worship, is it?

Back to the point at hand. A friend of mine struggled with harmful sexual relationships. Not long after, I casually mentioned what another friend was wearing. He claimed not to notice: "I'm not looking at women below the neck," he said. It sounds pious, even misogynistic. But his effort to re-train where he looked paid off, first in his treating women differently from before, and eventually in a happy marriage. We can train up our children, or retrain ourselves, in healthy ways. The desert tradition makes clear that the effort involved will be strenuous but promises it can be rewarding.

The more troublesome theme here is the personification of evil in the form of a "black" demon and then as a black woman (V.4 & V.23). We shall see later that Abba Moses's blackness is a source of questioning for the *Sayings*. Racism, in one sense, is not a new phenomenon. Yet this is not mod-ern racism, premised as it is on the inherent inferiority of a certain kind of person, and on a history of perpetual bondage and then segregation. The saying at hand is, more basely, our tendency to notice and classify according to superficial differ-ence. The stories about Moses challenge this tendency. Yet as these two sayings make clear, what we think of as "race" can be spoken of here in less than beneficial ways.

Finally, the penchant for the dramatic gesture is ever with the desert fathers. A "harlot" (another troublesome objectifi-cation, here on the basis of gender) takes it on herself to tempt a famous hermit. He lets her into his cell and to stave off lust says to himself, "The ways of the enemy are darkness, but the Son of God is light." Then he burns his fingers, not noticing the pain, we're told, because the passion in him burned even stronger. She's rightly horrified! And she's struck dead. Not to worry, though he's angry with her ("Look what the child of the devil has done to me. She has cost me every finger I possess!"), he restores her life, and she lives chastely (V.37). These people were serious! Above all about their sexual renunciation. The last saying of this section insists it is easier to stir up wars and natural disasters than it is to cause one monk to lust. And yet this very rigor is impossible and unintelligible without grace—grace which is impossible and unintelligible without severity. Perhaps the desert fathers can reunite that which has too often been severed in our day.

Questions

1. Do the troublesome aspects of these texts (say, their depiction of "blacks" or women or of sexuality generally) spoil any spiritual fruit we might have hoped to gather here? Why or why not?

2. The church is often charged with superciliousness in its views toward sex by a world that claims sex is not such a big deal. Is this a fair charge? Why would the desert fathers disagree?

3. Can you think of an instance in which someone's habits of attention have been so trained as to guide one to act differently in their sexual life? What about an instance in which such attempted training had adverse effects?

4. In these sayings does "mercy triumph over justice" (James 2:13)? Why or why not?

VI. Possessing Nothing

⅙ From the vantage of our own materialistically possessed age, the desert fathers' refusal of possessions may be even stranger than their giving up of sex or autonomy. They would respond to us that they are simply following the clear command of Jesus: "none of you can become my disciple if you do not give up all your possessions" (Luke 14:33). Far from being an isolated command of Jesus meant to put us in the right psychological frame of mind about our not-given-up possessions (how many have heard this sermon preached?: "Jesus doesn't mean for us to give up our stuff; he just means for us not to love it too much . . ."), this command was materially embodied in an ancient church for which dispossession was *the* sign of the Spirit's outpouring. Duke professor Richard Hays argues that Acts 2:43–44 is widely mistranslated.[1] It should read "many wonders and signs were being done by the apostles, *for* all who believed were together and had all things in common." Where I italicized *for* is normally a period. In the Greek the verse is clear: the signs and wonders of the apostles include, preeminently, the sharing of possessions. For the less linguistically attentive, Acts is clearer elsewhere: "Now the whole group of those who believed were of one heart and soul, and no one claimed private ownership of any possessions, but everything they owned was held in common" (4:32). A fringe minority of Christians throughout the church's history

1. Richard Hays, *The Moral Vision of the New Testament: A Contemporary Introduction to New Testament Ethics* (San Francisco: Harper, 1996) 123.

has taken the New Testament at its word and tried to live out possessionlessness. Such "experiments," we may call them, remain in Catholic and Orthodox monasteries, in Catholic Worker houses, and in Anabaptist communities such as the Bruderhoff in New York.[2]

The very first saying in this section shows the importance of dispossession in characteristically dramatic fashion. A monk who has learned the lesson of obedience, if not of possessing nothing, hears a word from Antony: rub meat on your naked body and come back. His flesh is torn by beasts. Then Antony says, "Those who renounce the world but want to keep their money are attacked in that way by demons and torn in pieces" (VI.1). In another combination of difficult saying with dramatic gesture, a hermit takes off his clothes, girds his loins, stretches his hands and says, "Thus ought the monk to be: stripped naked of everything, and crucified by temptation and combat with the world" (VI.16). How appealing! Yet, note the accent in the Antony story. It is not just on the mandate to dispossession, but on the graciousness of it. One who holds possessions back is torn apart; one who does not, presumably, is not. The second saying, perhaps more realistically, expresses the difficulty of dispossession, comparing it to crucifixion. Yet the former note remains: giving up of possessions is easier, a lighter yoke even, than maintaining or hoarding them.

As soon as we hear this sort of radical demand, we begin thinking of qualifying questions. What about possessions that edify? St. Francis, whose poverty made him famous and earned

2. See my article, "The New Monastics: Alternative Christian Communities," *Christian Century*, October 18, 2005.

him millions of imitators in the Middle Ages and since, kept a silver communion set as a way of honoring the one thing in life worthy of adornment. Yet is that not a possession? The same might be asked on behalf of monastic communities, one of whose prime gifts to the church and the world has been the preservation of learning. Especially in the ancient world in which a book was a luxury, should not the monks make exceptions to their austere search for poverty in the case of books? The monks have a set of surprisingly funny sayings to offer in response: "I have sold even the word that commands me to sell all and give to the poor" (VI.5). "Reading books is good, but possessing nothing is more than anything" (VI.6). These paradoxical formulations lead to more questions: how do we conduct worship without a Bible? One answer is that many ancient monastics memorized large portions, or even all, of the Scriptures. The second saying suggests that it would be fine for a community to possess a Bible if it is willing to settle for less than full holiness! Another saying expresses the presumption against book possession even more starkly: "'You have taken what belongs to widows and orphans and put it on your window-ledge.' He saw that the window-ledge was full of books" (VI.12). Of course, that the monks wrote down these very sayings suggests there was still some place for bibliophilia in their lives!

As comparing the goodness of books with the greatness of dispossession suggests, there is awareness in the sayings of a range of responses to Jesus' difficult commands. One of the desert mothers, Syncletica, is asked whether absolute poverty is perfect goodness. "It is a great good for those who can do it. Even those who cannot bear it find rest to their souls though they suffer bodily anxiety" (VI.13). Here only some can achieve perfect poverty. Those who cannot, paradoxically, suffer more than those who can. In any event, there is space in this and other sayings for some possessions but greater hallowing for their absence. One can think of contemporary parallels: my own education, blessing though I hope it is to myself and others, cost ghastly amounts of money during its thirteen-year tenure at private schools, nine years of which were in post-secondary education. It is a good thing, but poverty would have been better, for the desert fathers. The final saying here suggests as much again. A hermit allows a seeker to keep some coins for himself. The seeker finds no peace, however, so makes the hermit swear to tell the truth: "I told you to keep [the shillings] because I saw you intended to do so anyway. But it is not good to have more than the body needs" (VI.22). Here again, poverty is simply more blessed than possessions. As we have seen in previous chapters, there is need of a wise counselor who can apply precepts and advice with skill to particular persons and circumstances, filtering the presumption in favor of poverty through individual lives.

Even with this preference for dereliction, as we might call it, there is no blanket condemnation of commerce here. One monk worries as much: "What am I to do? I am anxious when I sell what I make." Pistamon replies, "There is no harm in this . . . If you want to lower the price a little, you may and so you will find peace" (VI.11). Business as such is not bad. In fact, it can be conducted in a manner that reflects the mercy of Christ. This is important for an ascetic life that was often (if meagerly!) fed by earnings from plaited rope the monks wove while praying. One can think here of, say, fair-trade coffee, or the organic farming materials Mepkin Abbey and other monasteries sell at its store and online.[3] Buying and selling as such is not necessarily sinful; it simply needs to be conducted in a way that reflects Jesus, as all things must for Christians.

There are also obvious dangers about dispossession. It can lead to pride, a sin worse than wealth. One monk worries here that if he is given wealth "when I would have given it to others, I would suffer from vanity" (VI.17). The other question is, naturally, where should the wealth go?[4] The (apocryphal?) story circulates among Roman Catholic religious about the father driving his son to the monastery he was to join. As they passed through the computerized gate onto the immaculate campus with its opulent buildings, the father said, "If this is poverty, I can't wait to see chastity!" That is to say, when individuals give up wealth, the church can become fabulously wealthy, a result not obviously intended in Scripture's admonitions to poverty. The *Sayings* are attuned to this worry.[5] A rich

3. My favorite: New Melleray Abbey in Dubuque, Iowa, will sell you a pine box in which to be buried, prayed over by the monk who made the box by hand. The elegance of these caskets is hard to believe, given their price tags of just under $2,000 each. (To spend this amount on arrangements would indeed run counter to the culture of our exorbitant funeral homes!) Trappist monks themselves, I am told, are buried without caskets. They are simply lowered into the ground in their habits, and those attending help to bury the brother.

4. This question brings to mind the oft-used vignette in youth group talks: that the backseat of a car is not the best place for young people to think about how far they're willing to go sexually!

5. The *Lives* perhaps even more so: Abba Theodore laments the economic success of his community, actually going out and praying with tears over the tomb of its founder, Pachomius. Harmless writes, "It did no good. The good order and efficient work habits of the *Koinonia* proved too successful—a pattern that would be repeated many times in the history of medieval monasticism" (137).

man carries gold to Scetis, where no one will accept it. The brothers tell him to carry it away to the poor (VI.19). Even giving it to the poor can have an unintended and deleterious consequence. Does Jesus merely wish for the poor to become rich? Then his harsh words of judgment for the rich would simply fall upon them—not an obvious improvement! Again, the *Sayings* suggest as much. One leper refuses an offer of alms by showing his abundance: "I have a few palm leaves to work, and I plait them, and so I get enough to eat." A daughter of a widow refuses alms for the same reason. The mother is even more adamant: "I have my God to care for me. Do you want to take him away from me now?" (VI.18). Another leper sounds a similar tune, "Are you going to take me away from Him who has fed me for sixty years?" (VI.20). The potential for abuse of this tradition, of offering pious platitudes to the poor when they need food and shelter, or of leaving unjust wealth horded while lecturing the needy, is obvious (James 2:14–17). Yet the point, to us counterintuitive, is instructive: to give someone any amount of wealth is not obviously to have done them a favor.

The heart of this portion of the desert tradition is about God and human trust. The question it asks is whether our trust is in God or elsewhere, with little middle ground between the two would-be objects of trust. We have here a radically despiritualized, and quite material, ethical vision: Christians cannot claim their trust is in God if they have enough money to trust in that, whatever their attitude toward such money may be. When Satan invites a brother to "Store up a little money, as a provision to spend when you are old and infirm" (VI.21), we naturally think of our society's coveting of retirement pensions and health insurance. The man falls ill and does not recover until he gives up his store of coins, at which point he is miraculously cured. In these stories about the conflict between trust in divine provision and trust in every other sort of provision, we hear echoed Jesus' insistence, "Where your treasure is, there your heart will be also" (Matt 6:21).

Questions

1. Is this the hardest of the many hard practices of the desert fathers to imagine living out? Why or why not?

2. What further problems do you see with divestment of all property? What potential gains?

3. Is there anything to be said for the softening of these biblical commands along these lines: "Jesus doesn't mean to give up all possessions, he just intends us to keep them in proper perspective"?

4. Is it possible to take small steps toward "possessing nothing" in the more mundane hope of possessing less? What might some such steps be?

VII. Fortitude

❦ An easy misconception in reading the desert literature is to imagine the ascetic life as exciting. Stories about duels and wisecracks with demons, or encounters with archbishops, or dramatic gestures, could lead to the taking up of desert monasticism as a sort of thrill seeking. If we are tempted to this, this section is a tonic. "They said of Sarah of blessed memory that for sixty years she lived on the bank of a river, and never looked at the water" (VII.19). The point of the saying is obvious enough: a studied habit of attention upon God and the right ordering of desire for him. Yet, the obvious question arises, was that *all* she did? Abba Ammonas, one of the greats of the desert, said he spent fourteen years in Scetis asking God for help in controlling his temper (VII.3). Theodore of Pherme rebukes a monk for thinking eight years should have been enough to achieve peace. "Believe me, I've been a monk for seventy years, and I've not been able to get a single day's peace. Do you expect to have peace after only eight years?" (VII.5). It is clear that whatever pious tourism or spiritual thrill seeking many of us conduct in our search for spiritual learning, it is precisely the penchant for spiritual adventure that the desert fathers seek quickly to root out of their souls.

The first step toward stability of spirit is dedication to stability of place. Amma Syncletica, expressing the same preference for rootedness as her sister Sarah, said, "The monk or nun who goes from place to place grows cold and dead in faith" (VII.15). Two brothers, Theodore and Lucius, keep each other stable by convincing themselves they should stay one season, until they spent half a century dedicated to a single place (VII.7). More disturbing, an unusually long saying suggests a monk ought not even leave the cell for the sacrament (VII.24). Yet another does give some conditions under which a monk should move: anger that cannot be assuaged, lust, or excessive praise (!) (VII.26). We have seen other sayings that suggest remedies for each of these problems, so the burden of proof is clearly on moving. In one encounter, we can imagine a spiritual thrill seeker the likes of which Athanasius's *Life of Antony* sent to the desert by the thousand: "What am I to do, abba? I do nothing like a monk. I eat, drink and sleep as I like, I am much troubled by vile thoughts, I shift from task to task, and my mind wanders everywhere." The response: "Stay in your cell, and do what you can without anxiety. It is not much that you do now, yet it is the same as when Antony did mighty things in the desert" (VII.34). Impressive as the accounts of great spiritual feats are, a yoke to the place of one's cell is greater still.[1]

And what was one to do in the cell, all day, for decades? Work. Abba Mathois says, "I like to find some light but con-

---

1. Since monks' pledge to a particular place, and a particular cell, I am impressed by the faithfulness with which they respond to their orders' requests for them to move elsewhere, for example to start new monasteries. Br. Joseph, the "liturgical guestmaster" at Mepkin Abbey of whom I spoke above, promised to live out his days at Gethsemani in Kentucky, before being asked to move to low country South Carolina. The monks at Holy Cross Monastery in Chicago originally pledged to be present at Christ in the Desert Monastery in Abiqui, New Mexico—quite a shift, that one! Holy Cross's website trades on the infamous television series *Sex and the City* with its own slogan: "Silence in the City"! Perhaps the line between monastic kitsch and more genuine spiritual practice is blurred by the monasteries themselves!

tinual work, rather than a heavy work that is quickly finished" (VII.11). Another monk who is tempted with the thought that any action is sinful is told to stay in his cell. After three days, he "begins" to get bored! So he makes plaits for a few days. When he's hungry, he does a few more before eating. Then, a few more, putting off food still longer. In this way, by pledging to work "just a bit longer," hunger is overcome (VII.27). As other sayings make clear, the point is less on the stamping out of all physical desire, like hunger. It is more a studied attention to the task at one's hand, in this case plaiting, accompanied as it was by prayer, without attending to the next task even if it is to satisfy a basic bodily need.

This work—menial weaving of plaits, for example—was not easily distinguishable from prayer. The mental quiet that comes with rote work opens the way to attention to the sorts of temptations we all face. Hyperichius therefore counsels, "Keep praising God with hymns, meditating continually, and so lighten the burden of the temptations that attack you" (VII,20). Another saying counsels a Psalm verse as a sort of tonic for each of several particular temptations (VII.16). In short, the sort of work the fathers sought stills the soul, allows an arena for the struggle against temptation, and finally clears space for communion with God and others. When two greats, Macarius and Antony, finally meet, after Antony closes the door in Macarius's face, they simply make plaits together all night. After their conversationless exchange, Antony kisses Marcaius's hand and says, "there is great virtue in those plaits." The physical object stands for, and in a sense *is*, progress in prayer and so communion with others. Words need not pass for friendship where prayer is present.

As ever, what we see here both compels and repels. For even illness can be treated as something "deserved," for which gratitude can be given—a posture that opens the way for the grotesque sight of thanking God for cancer or AIDS (see VII.17 & VII.41). Yet we also see a compelling plea for permanence in commitment, avoidance of superficial entertainment, and pursuit of genuine love. The monks cannot have imagined the sort of instant society in which we live, with its promise of communication without delay and saturation with entertainment. A visit to Alexandria was temptation enough for them! When we try to achieve quiet we have almost to detoxify from noise, accustomed to it as we are. After a few moments' discomfort in quiet, we are inclined to check e-mail again. At least the troubled desert monastic was only bored after three days! Then, once quiet is achieved, temptations and troubling thoughts can be patiently dealt with, praised- and prayed-through. Finally, a quiet is achieved in which the Spirit of God prays in us, through us, even with others, without words (Rom 8:26).[2] Decades are required for this sort of learning about interior affection, exterior attention, and patient love. We see this in one monk's effort to be cured of anger by becoming a hermit. He smashes a jug that refuses to stay still and only then realizes that *he* is the problem: "Here I am by myself, and [Satan] has beaten me. I will return to

2. Sarah Coakley has written beautifully about the importance of wordless prayer in the formulation and maintenance of a full-fledged doctrine of the Trinity, in such places as "Living into the Mystery of the Holy Trinity: Trinity, Prayer, and Sexuality," *Anglican Theological Review* 80 (1998) 223–32; and "Why Three? Some Further Reflections on the Origins of the Doctrine of the Trinity," in *The Making and Remaking of Christian Doctrine: Essays for Maurice Wiles*, ed. Sarah Coakley and David A. Pailin (New York: Oxford University Press, 1993) 29–54.

the community" (VII.33). Years are required for our almost innate selfishness to rise to the surface sufficiently in order to be seen in ugly, stark relief, and trimmed away, for genuine life in Christian community.

And then, maybe then, we can speak again in terms that will sound like spiritual thrill seeking. For example, the fourth, angelic figure in the fiery furnace in Daniel 3 is actually Jesus. Jesus is seen in the cell like the fourth, angel-like figure in the fiery furnace in the story in Daniel 3 (VII.38). In accordance with ancient Christian allegorical exegesis of the Bible, this Old Testament story, with its embodiment of divine presence, is thought to prefigure the incarnation. The message is clear: stay in the fire of the cell long enough, and you will see the fiery one who protects and saves. Precisely this sort of tedious, mind-numbing quiet and rootage to a place is required to pursue Jesus as a hound pursues a hare, aiming "unceasingly at the cross, and leap[ing] over every obstacle in his way until he comes to the Crucified" (VII.35).

The *Sayings* do hold out promise of exciting dueling with demons, as in the case of Macarius's brazen decision to sleep in a pagan cemetery. The demons try to frighten him by speaking from the corpse of the mummy on which he sleeps. "Get up and go if you can," Macarius taunts. The demons flee (VII.10). This line, that we inevitably hear delivered with the sort of snarl with which a Schwarzenegger or an Eastwood dispatches a bad guy, actually bespeaks a sort of studied indifference to spiritual malady. One who has faced the terror of temptation within will have no fear from such silly exterior temptation as a little demon can muster from a graveyard. Such is the fruit of decades of weaving plaits and firing Scripture at thoughts that threaten peace.

Questions

1. Paul Griffiths writes of the omnipresence of lying in our politics and consumer culture and commends the church's ancient (but often forgotten) practices of silence as a tonic.[3] Does silence become more attractive as speech seems more commonly duplicitous? Why or why not?

2. Where have you found space for silence? Anywhere particularly surprising? Has rote work ever helped you pray?[4] Or does silence simply terrify?

3. How might silence be an answer to our culture's common acceptance of lies?

4. Is there a place for spiritual thrill-seeking after all, or is that always dangerous?

---

3. Griffiths, *Lying*, 229.

4. My own best "silence" comes on the commuter train in the mornings. Despite loud train noise and other passengers' shouting into cell phones, I find "space" here, away from my own phone and e-mail, to pray.

Coakley has also written about the subversive nature of teaching prisoners wordless prayer. It undoes one of the rubrics of dehumanization behind bars—the constant noise ("Jail break: Meditation as a subversive activity," *Christian Century*, June 29, 2004, 18–21).

VIII. Nothing Done for Show

✠ There is a tension at the heart of the *Sayings* not unlike that at the heart of Augustine's *Confessions*. The tension can be expressed in a question: How can Augustine say that pride is the worst of sins and then proceed to write so much about himself? Similarly, the desert fathers sought to escape the world's common forms of social recognition and esteem. Yet they allowed their sayings and deeds to be recorded and were acquainted enough with visitors who had heard of their fame to know that these *Sayings* would be read far and wide. How does one submit to ever more austere forms of self-abnegation and also tell others about one's holiness so as to invite imitators? Even the solitude-seeking hermits read the Scriptures that call for community and insist on God's mandate to encourage others to holiness.

This section of the *Sayings* wrestles with this paradox of despising but gaining fame. Its solutions are, not surprisingly, severe. Monks ought to hate praise and fame more than anything (VIII.3). They ought not even seek to *sit* with famous men (VIII.5). Showiness about holiness yields crowds and so ought to be avoided for that reason (VIII.11). Abba Poemen will not even relent to see a judge when he has his nephew arrested! (VIII.13). It is far better to fool a monastic "groupy," as we might call them, by pretending to be someone else, or pretending to be sinful, or pretending no such person exists. As the great Abba Moses asks an entourage that had come to

65

see him, "What do you want to see him for? He's a fool and a heretic" (VIII.10).

Here we see that monks wish to flee fame perhaps even more than they wish to flee women and bishops. Not only because fame disturbs their prayer, but because of its spiritual effect upon them. Celebrity can be intoxicating, as our culture's fascination with entertainers makes clear. Being an intoxicant for others can be even more dangerous, as our entertainers' personal lives splayed out in tabloids make abundantly clear.[1] Even in more ecclesial professions, ministers fall, seminary professors abuse, spiritual guides mislead. For the esteem that students and children rightly hold for their leaders can so easily be mistaken for worship directed at that person in her own right and so can contort self-perception and the relationship as a whole.

I myself contrast the monks' prescriptions with my own behavior toward "famous" people (an odd and small sliver of the general populace: those well known in theology and church circles). I like to get to know them, figuring such people are more impressed by someone who will challenge them than someone who slinks back in cautious admiration. There is much to learn from conversation with a well-regarded cleric or scholar after all. Not to mention that such a relation might prove advantageous down the road! Or in my position as a writer, I live for moments when people recognize my name, or even say my work has meant something to them. "I must be worth something after all," I think, since at least he thinks so.

---

1. The thought is not original to me, but it is striking the degree to which one cannot avoid knowing the intimate details of entertainers' lives. There is a sort of violence in the fact that Whoever's latest sexual escapades shout in the face of anyone who goes to buy food at the grocery store.

Notice what happens here: persons are reduced to commodities, esteem is sought in achievement rather than in Scripture's story of sin and redemption, and ego trumps divine presence. The monks were wise to give no quarter to such thoughts.

Even here, there is more going on than mere renunciation of the world, important though that is. There is also a recognition of the importance of Christian community, even for desert ascetics. They did disseminate their words and deeds after all, convinced that by imitating them others would imitate Christ (1 Cor 11:1). A bishop (warning!) visited the great Sisois, who had, unbeknownst to the bishop, been fasting many days. Without warning, the hermit breaks bread for and with the bishop, scandalizing his followers. So his followers told the bishop: "God forgive you letting him eat at this hour. Don't you know he has been fasting rigorously for many days?" (VIII.15). Sisois's reaction is telling: "Unless God glorifies man, man's glory cannot last." That is, fame before another falls to dust in the face of "fame" before God. In another case, a monk calls attention to the fact that he eats nothing cooked, only salted. He receives his rebuke: "It would have been better for you to eat meat today in your cell than to have heard this said in front of many brothers" (VIII.21). Self-regard is a ravenous vice, consuming interactions with others, prayer, even God. The desert was a laboratory for training *out* of undue self-regard and *into* proper regard for God and others. Praise was more dangerous for the success of that experiment than almost anything. That was the key message the monks attempted to pass on to the world, as part of becoming less for the sake of One who would become greater in them.

Questions

1. How does one solve the contradiction between monks' desire to avoid "fame" and their "success" in spiritual matters,
success that necessarily draws others to want their advice
and company? Is Abba Moses's comment to the one seeking him right: "What do you want to see him for? He's a
fool and a heretic"? Or does that display a strange "pride"
of sorts—an unwillingness to be present to help another
part of the body of Christ seek sanctification?

2. How might we rearrange our priorities so we are less attentive to "famous" people and more attentive to, say, the
poor?

3. Is there a danger here of undue *in*attention to the self or others? Or, is that hardly a problem in our self-absorbed age?

IX. Nonjudgement

✢ Here we see the desert fathers in their full glory. If anyone should have the right to judge another, it should be these desert monastics, whose entire lives were devoted to the pursuit of rigorous holiness. And yet, when a monk is removed from the assembly, Abba Bessarion goes as well, for he says, "I, too, am a sinner" (IX.2). Abba Moses is summoned to an assembly to judge another, and perhaps having learned from the cruelty with which he was often treated for his skin color, he offers a dramatic demonstration. He piles sand into a basket on his back, walks to the assembly, and says, "My sins run out behind me and I do not see them and I have come here today to judge another" (IX.4, 9).

Another saying focuses on an issue that troubled North African Christian communities for many years—the holiness (or lack thereof) of certain priests. During the persecutions of the church that took place sporadically in the late third and early fourth centuries, priests as well as lay Christians often apostatized—that is, they renounced their faith, handed over copies of the Scriptures to Roman authorities, and did whatever else was necessary to avoid martyrdom. The question was, what should the church do with them after the persecution was lifted and their treachery discovered? Worse, what is to be thought of those sacraments they had once performed? If it turned out that the priest by whom one had been baptized or married was really an apostate, what validity is there to that baptism or marriage? Should it be done anew? This issue would vex Augustine somewhat later than the desert fathers and a bit to the east of Scetis, and his answer would satisfy the rest of the church indefinitely: a sacrament is valid because of the grace of God rather than the goodness of the priest.

So too here. Monks would be as likely as anyone to worry scrupulously about the holiness of the administrator of their sacraments. What if that one turned out to be a sinner? In a vision, a hermit sees "a well of gold and a bucket of gold, and a rope of gold, and plenty of drinking water. He saw a leper emptying and refilling the bucket" and so does not drink. The point: "What does it matter who draws [the water]?" It is, after all, drawn with gold, whoever does the lifting. So, too, should Christians see the preciousness of the sacrament, whatever the spiritual state of the hands that carry it (IX.11).

The final saying in this section suggests that grace is almost physical, and its presence detectible by another. A brother says a mildly judgmental thing to another about fasting, and his friend asks, "What have you done, brother? I do not see the grace of God in you as I used to." Upon investigation, the word about fasting is remembered, the two do penance *together* for two weeks, "and they were comforted, and gave thanks to God who alone is good."

Questions

1) What does a dramatic display of the teaching that "mercy triumphs over judgment" (James 2:13) accomplish that merely quoting the verse does not?

2) Can one *see* holiness? Is there a specific instance in which you have?

X. Discretion

❦ Monastic life was and is not the same for all those who seek it. There is no mechanistic formula for how to be a "good" or "bad" monk, extraordinary as it seems to say that. For as rigorous as the desert fathers were, they were also fully aware that there are as many ways to be a monk as there are creatures made by God and willing to seek such a life. Therefore, a spiritual advisor needs to be skillful in "discretion," that is, in knowing how to apply what spiritual teaching to whom and in what way. The analogy here is that of a medical doctor. She must know all the potential cures at her disposal, with all the technical skill necessary to know their possible applications. But medicine is not formulaic. She must also know how to "read" her patients to know what should be applied and how. So, too, with directing novices in the spiritual life. Those advanced in the spiritual life of the desert had to know how to apply what advice to which novice and how. This task is as crucial as it is difficult.[1]

1. The illustration is a venerable one in the history of the church, dating back at least to Origen: "As every herb has its own virtue whether for the healing of the body, or some other purpose, and it is not given to everybody to know the use of every herb. . . . The saint is a sort of spiritual herbalist, who culls from the sacred Scriptures every jot and every common letter. . . . Just so you may regard the Scriptures as a collection of herbs, or as one perfect body of reason; but if you are [not] a scriptural botanist . . . you must not suppose that anything written is superfluous. See *Philocalia of Origen, A Compilation of Selected Passages from Origen's Works Made by St. Gregory of Nazianzus and St. Basil of Caesaria*, trans. George Lewis (Edinburgh: T. & T. Clark, 1911) X.2, 52.

Daniel tells the story from Arsenius about a brother who would steal. Arsenius tried first to treat this kleptomania with the standard monastic approach of giving him what he wanted. Yet when the brother would not stop stealing, he had to be expelled, for "he hurts his own soul, and also disturbs everyone who lives here" (X.18). We see here two different portions of the biblical tradition at work. One is the demand for radical forgiveness, dispossession of property, and creative desire to win over the brother, all of which become central to the desert monastic tradition. The other is the "limit" of the community's grace. In severe cases a church member must be cast out for the sake of the whole body's health and ultimately for the sake of his also (see, e.g., Matthew 18:15–20 and 1 Corinthians 5:1–13). Rowan Williams says in *God's Advocates* that the "New Testament is a work in progress."[2] That is, the New Testament is not a set of abstract principles that can be applied bloodlessly to all situations. It is rather a jumble of difficult and competing messages that must be skillfully woven together in response to particular difficulties in life. Christian living is, in short, a matter of "practical wisdom," of knowing how to apply what virtue to each circumstance in the right way. Here Jesus' call to radical forgiveness is applied—to a point.

Other sayings in this section show the need for discretion in a way that puzzles onlookers. Two monks with good reputations fail to get a keepsake from the great Achillas. But another with a poor reputation convinces the abba to make him a fishing net. Why? "If I did not do it for this monk,

2. Interview with author Rupert Shortt, *God's Advocates: Christian Thinkers in Conversation* (Grand Rapids: Eerdmans, 2005) 1.

he would say, 'The hermit has heard my reputation and for that reason has refused to make me a net.' So immediately I set out with the string, to soothe his soul and prevent him being sad" (X.14). Notice, this reverses our normal expectation that those who do well, or in this case are holier, will be rewarded more amply. Concerned about the damage that his meeting such a "normal" expectation would do the lesser monk, the abba acts on this monk's behalf rather than the others'. Likewise, Poemen is scandalized when Joseph gives advice to another monk in Poemen's hearing that is diametrically opposed to the advice that Joseph had just given him. The second monk is told not even to let temptation into his mind, whereas Poemen can notice the temptation and then send it away. The reason for the difference in advice is that the abba has determined the one monk can handle temptation or even use it to grow in holiness, and that the other can't and so should block it out entirely. How to tell? Discretion. This is not divination of a spiritual secret of some kind. It is wisdom born of patient and gentle attention to another and a desire to see that one thrive. A confessor has done the necessary work to perceive the other's needs and respond appropriately, without a one-size-fits all approach to spiritual living. In an even more stark example, a powerful passion like anger can be unilaterally condemned in one instance (X.13) and can be given a significant place in another (X.47). This is no more contradictory than the observation that two medicines can react differently in two different people. It is born of a sensitivity to making diagnosis that is necessary for directing others toward cure. "When Silvanus learnt what had been done, he acted like a skilled physician and put on his soul a poultice made of texts from scripture" (X.88).

If there is a guiding thread in these sayings about discretion (not a formula, but a standard of wisdom), it seems to be to err on the side of gentleness. For a community built and premised upon extraordinary spiritual rigor, these monks could be astoundingly gracious with the failures of their fellows. For instance, a monk is hell-bent on a heroic penance of three years. Poemen protests its length. One year? Another protest. Forty days, a good biblical number? Still, too long. "I think that if someone is whole-heartedly penitent, and determined not to sin that sin again, God will accept a penance of even three days" (X.40). Another monk is unable to do even basic monastic tasks like facing temptation, working, or giving alms. One would think his future in the desert would be bleak indeed. Not so for Brother Joseph: "If you cannot do any of these, at least keep your conscience clear from every sin against your neighbor, and you will be saved, for God looks for the soul that does not sin" (X.31). In an echo of the gospel tradition about the Pharisees, Poemen says that one's own sins are like the great beam that holds up a house, and the other's sins are like a tiny piece of straw ignored on the ground (X.37).

In fact, the only occasion that seems not to call for exquisite gentleness from the *Sayings* is the appearance of pride, expressed either in the prescription of heroic spiritual activity for oneself or in discouraging evaluation that saddens another. One monk so discourages another that he almost sends him back to the world muttering, "If I'm going to perish, I'll go and do it in the world." But a third monk, "who possessed great discretion," speaks gently and more scripturally to the dejected brother, winning him back (X.88). Even more poignantly, "If you see a young man climbing up to heaven by his own will, catch him by the foot and pull him down to earth for it is not good for him" (X.114). Longinus provides an example of this pulling down to earth in response to Lucius's claims that he would go on a pilgrimage, fast for days, and avoid all company of others. He should instead control his tongue, guard from evil thoughts, and live among others (X.33). The spiritual life is about attention to small but good spiritual tasks now, rather than about making enormous promises that cannot be kept and that would cause pride even if they were. One thinks here of the promises we often make at Lent or New Year to run miles every day, which soon collapse. But attention to the exercise necessary to walk to the car, or to converse with a loved one, could bring humble gratitude and the chance for greater things.

One of the *Sayings'* funniest moments is in this section on discretion. The great John the Short goes off to be free of trouble like the angels, so he leaves his brothers. "After a week [alone], he went back to his brother." His brother cannot help but have a little fun with him before he accepts him anew. "'John has become an angel, and is no longer among men.' But he went on knocking and saying, 'It really is John'." The other brother eventually lets John in and reminds him that, in biblical parlance, one must work in order to eat. If we were angels, we would indeed be able to avoid such quotidian matters as food, drink, and one another. But, alas, we cannot, and so God has deigned to be graciously present even in such potentially difficult, potentially joyful matters as the stuff of daily life.

Questions

1. Is there a danger of "discretion" becoming an excuse for moral laxity? How might this be avoided?

2. How do Protestants, without a formal tradition of confession to another, put discretion to work?

3. What place does humor have in spiritual direction of other souls?

4. How does one become a person of discretion?

XI. Sober Living

❧ The closest neighbor we have to ancient Christian asceticism may be athletic training. Think of the extraordinary preparation Lance Armstrong had to put in to win the *Tour de France* with such regularity. I know a retired MI-5 agent from England who is now in his seventies who still, first thing in the morning, pops out of bed and does 150 push-ups. He can also deflect a knife thrust aimed at his chest just by flexing his pectoral muscles (or so I'm told). Or think of the legions of joggers outside your window daily. Wherever you live in the United States there will be people who, like St. Paul, "beat my body and make it my slave" for the sake of some greater end (1 Cor 9:27). Here, that end is often an impossible model of thinness.

The desert fathers sought to pour equally serious exertion into their efforts to desire God fully. Not unlike physical athletes, the fathers exerted both physical effort and emotional diligence to direct their entire attention toward a difficult goal: seeking God in all things. Metaphors of vision are extremely important in this endeavor: "When he was dying, Bessarion said, 'A monk ought to be like the Cherubim and Seraphim, all eye'" (XI.7). They did not wish merely to have their bodies perform certain ways, though that was important. They wished their minds and their souls to be directed toward God and away from sin. Lewis Ayres, a church historian at Candler School of Theology, speaks of the desert fathers seeking "certain patterns of attention" to God.[1] Described negatively, the monks thought of Christians as those who are constantly under attack from demons: "We ought to be armed at all points against the demons. They come at us from outside and if the soul is weak we invite them in" (XI.33). All of us have a constant stream of thoughts running through our mind's eye. Even before the information age, persons' memories shuttled bits of the past, fantasies, images of all sorts before them. For the monks, these images could be easily used by demons to pry their attention away from their own sin, God's grace, and the community that rehabilitates us out of the former and into the latter.

The physical requirements for developing gracious habits of attention are stern indeed. There is Silvanus covering his head with his hood so as to see nothing before him, lest his eyes be distracted by the thought even of a tree (XI.28). Here is Serapion commending imperial guards who turn their heads neither to the left nor to the right, an impressive physical feat (XI.31). Yet another commends a donkey's covered eyes while it works at the wheel (XI.49). This quite bodily infliction of right habits of attention is the context in which to read a saying like that of father Allois: "Until you can say in your heart, 'Only I and God are in the world,' you will not be at peace" (XI.5). At its worst, this sounds like so much selfishness, like the kind of sin against which monks flee into the desert in the first place! At its best, it sounds like a kind of spiritual bluster, a claim to climb toward God without the aid of other people, against which the *Sayings* rightly rail elsewhere (X.114). It

1. Lewis Ayres, "On the Practice and Teaching of Christian Doctrine," *Gregorianum* 80 (1999) 33–94.

reads better, however, as another admonition to pay strict attention to God first, and to all other people and things only in light of God. For even quite good things, such as food and drink and prayer and fellowship, can be used by the demons to pry attention away from God. This is sober advice indeed. Even with our best efforts, without God's grace we should be lost (XI.11)

Yet this advice needn't be simply dreary, as this set of sayings makes clear. Blessed John once accidentally wove strands from two baskets into one and did not notice until he went to hang the basket(s?) up, for his mind was so absorbed in contemplation of God (XI.14). In another instance, a monk asks for the grace to become sleepy when anyone speaks ill but to be avidly attentive when speech is directed toward God. (As a preacher, I can tell you most of those who sit in pews need to say this prayer with some regularity.) When he noticed novices growing sleepy during his discourse about God, he turned to gossip, at which point they perked up! (XI.18). The story illustrates the key point: our desires are all backwards. We value the valueless and despise the priceless. We ought rather be more like the monk in the other humorous story, who walks all the way home trying to remember his question for the abba, remembers the question once his key is in his door, and then returns to the abba at once, leaving the key jutting out. The spiritual life is so vital, so crucial, that its pursuit will have us do things that seem absentminded to observers. In reality they signal our primary attention to the one thing worthy of our mind's observance.

By itself this description could suggest an individualistic spirituality, a claim that we should pull ourselves up by our bootstraps to God. To speak more theologically, it would fit with what Sarah Coakley calls "a sweaty Pelagianism," a view that if we work as hard as we can, God may deign to reward us.[2] When the desert fathers sound that way, it is important to read other sayings about their love for Christian community. These very sayings were remembered, written down, and treasured for centuries as aids to help create future Christian community. Poemen makes this point clear in retelling a memory of a question put to Paesius: "'What am I to do about my soul? I have become incapable of feeling and I do not fear God.' He said to him, 'Go, and live with someone who does fear God: and by being there, you too will learn to fear God'" (XI.23). We *are* the company we keep.

We are also our memories. Poemen here reaches into the past and creates a sort of mythic group memory about Paesius's efforts to help another monk, all as part of helping us, future readers and pray-ers. It might seem counterintuitive to say that these great athletes of the spiritual life were really about the creation of faithful community, for they sought individual cells in the desert to get away from people, after all! Yet in this story about John the Short, we can see it is so: A young monk cannot remember the advice John gives. So he constantly returns to him. This could be dangerous, not only because the hermit seeks solitude, but because pestering by someone who wants wisdom could itself lead to pride, or at least to great annoyance! John responds with extraordinary gentleness. He has the monk light a lamp, and then other lamps from that one, to show that light is not diminished by its passing on. "In the same way, John would not be harmed if

2. Coakley, "The Eschatological Body," 62.

all the monks of Scetis should come to me, it would not keep me from God's love. So come to me whenever you want, and don't hesitate" (XI.15). In this way, we are told, the monk's memory was cured! This is no trivial matter; our memory of both past misdeeds and faithful examples allows us to imagine future faithful possibilities.

Then we see this extraordinary conclusion: "This was the work of the hermits of Scetis, to strengthen those who were attacked by passion; their experience in conflict with themselves meant that they were able to help others along the way." Not a bad description of Christian life in any time and place.

Questions

1. Is my heavy accent on the monks' love of community perhaps too strong in light of sayings such as that in XI.5 ("Allois said, 'Until you can say in your heart, "Only I and God are in the world," you will not be at peace'")?

2. What can we learn from the analogy between contemporary athletes and the desert fathers? Are such examples overused in our time and so no longer of much help?

XII. Unceasing Prayer

☙ How exactly is one to keep St. Paul's admonition to "pray without ceasing" (1 Thess 5:17)? Presumably one must also eat, sleep, work, and do perhaps any number of other things! Yet the sayings are full of stories of monks who seem to do just that—to pray without ceasing—to a supernatural degree. Arsenius would begin prayer at sundown and not stop until sunrise (XII.1). Impressive, but not supernatural yet. In another case, a brother is asked why a drought will not relent in the face of prayer. "'I don't think you are praying earnestly enough. . . .' He stretched out his hands to heaven and prayed; and at once rain fell. The brother was afraid at the sight, and fell down and worshipped" (XII.14). Or this, perhaps the most impressive saying in the entire collection: "The hermit stood up and spread out his hands toward heaven, and his fingers shone like ten flames of fire, and he said, 'If you will, you can become all flame'" (XII.8). Lovely as that image is, it makes it sound as though those of us whose fingers rarely turn into flames simply lack the will.

Yet elsewhere in this section, we find a much more circumspect description of the difficulty of prayer: "I may be wrong but I think nothing needs so much effort as prayer to God" (XII.2). In my own efforts to pray while visiting monasteries, I have found this to be the case. After my standard half-hour set of prayers for my own needs, for my family, for my friends, for the church, and for the world, I'm out of things to say! And that's when I take what is for me an extraordinary amount of time, far more than in an ordinary day. We find here advice for us who are relative novices when it comes to prayer: "There is no need to talk much in prayer. Reach out your hands often, and say, 'Lord have mercy on me, as you will and as you know.' But if conflict troubles you, say, 'Lord, help me.' He knows what is best for us, and has mercy" (XII.10). As Anne Lamott likes to say, all her prayers can be reduced to either "Help me! Help me! Help me!" or "Thank you! Thank you! Thank you!"[1]

Here again we see the paradoxes in the *Sayings*: one, a call for heroic, supernatural feats of prayer; the other, a recognition of how difficult prayer is for most of us ordinary people. And here again, the resolution between the competing portions of the *Sayings* is in Christian community. Most of us, even most desert monastics, would look at Abba Joseph's fiery fingers and feel their own tips turn cold. But this is not a competition. We needn't feel envious of another's proximity to God and its extraordinary physical manifestations. We can instead be glad that one among us, even if a long time ago, could throw prayer around like fire. In the "communion of the saints" that creed-saying Christians confess, we belong to one Joseph, whose fiery prayers presumably are prayed also now for us. There is between him and us almost infinite possibility for growth in prayer, between our frequent experience of chill and the possibility of flame demonstrated in his flesh.

Further, the *Sayings* themselves resolve this tension with their common move of a turn toward Christian community. Lucius rebukes those who proudly claim they pray without

1. Anne Lamott, *Traveling Mercies: Some Thoughts on Faith* (Anchor, 2000) 82.

ceasing, since they also eat and sleep. Then he tells them his solution to the conflict between bodily needs and Scriptural admonition: "When I spend all day working and praying in my heart, I make about sixteen pence. Two of these I put outside the door, and with the rest I buy food. Whoever finds the two pennies outside the door prays for me while I am eating and sleeping: and so by God's grace I fulfill the text, 'Pray without ceasing'" (XII.9). We have an echo here of the venerable Christian tradition by which the poor need coins from the wealthy, and the wealthy need the prayers of the poor. We also have what looks to be rather foolish "investment" in worldly terms. Yet it is more important to the monk to have fulfilled the command to pray constantly than it is to save or spend more wisely. Here, the collision between our limits and the command combine in a cleverly faithful way to make possible unceasing prayer with an assumed reliance on others in the community, or on strangers. With a little help from others, "we," all in the body of Christ, can indeed pray without ceasing, with prayers that send our fingertips aflame.

Questions

1. Do you have examples of surprisingly faithful ways to "pray without ceasing"?

2. Have you ever had fingertips aflame? (I trust that we have all experienced digits of ice!)

3. With the exception of XII.14 ("'I don't think you are praying earnestly enough . . .' He stretched out his hands to heaven and prayed; and at once rain fell"), very few of these sayings suggest extraordinary "return" in response to prayer, only extraordinary exertion by the one praying. Why is that, do you suppose?

XIII. Hospitality

❧ The welcoming of strangers has always been at the heart of monastic life. In my own experience at the monastery, I found the monks warm and inviting, if not necessarily chatty or effusive. They showed me to a comfortable but hardly luxurious room, fed me healthy but not extravagant meals, and let me have an intimate part in the heart of their life—their worship. I never ceased to be amazed at Brother Joseph, the "liturgical guestmaster," as he would totter over to my stall and make sure I had the right service book open to the right page. That is, someone so devoted to worship as to give up the rest of his life to it, would interrupt his worship to be sure a visiting Protestant could sing along. The reason: Scripture speaks of guests as angels, or even as Jesus. By receiving visitors as Abraham did (those who came to him under the Oaks of Mamre), many have entertained angels unawares (so Heb 13:2; after Gen 18:1–15). Or as Jesus himself said, "I was a stranger, and you welcomed me" (Matt 25:35). This heavy emphasis on reception of the guest has led to some strange monastic visitors. During World War II, for example, monasteries were one place that refugee Jews could hide out from the Nazis without having questions asked or giving up their cover. Then after the war, some of those same Nazis could use monastic hospitality on the way to their escape to South America.

We can see the impetus to hospitality here in the *Sayings* in the way it conflicts with other ascetic commitments like fasting. What is a monk to do if a visitor appears on a fast day? The number of sayings here dedicated to the question suggests it was an important one. Yet the answer here is rather more unequivocal than it is on other disputed questions: hospitality is more important than the integrity of a fast. This is not merely because it is important to be nice. The insistence upon hospitality is rooted in profound reflection on the incarnation itself. When Cassian is asked about the question, he says, "Fasting is always possible but I cannot keep you [that is, guests] here forever. Fasting is useful and necessary, but we can choose to fast or not fast. God's law demands from us perfect love. I receive Christ when I receive you, so I must do all I can to show you love" (XIII.2). He then quotes Jesus' response when John the Baptist's disciples accusingly asked him why he did not fast (Matt 9:15). Fasting is done not in the bridegroom's presence at the wedding feast but after he is gone. The gospel writer may have meant that fasting was appropriate after Jesus' death, but the monastic writer knows better. Jesus *is* present in the monastic visitor, fasting is disallowed, and feasting is mandated.

Elsewhere an angry hermit insists that guests eat with him: "I have already given meals to six different visitors, and have eaten with each of them, and I am still hungry. And you who have only eaten once are so full that you cannot eat with me now?" (XIII.3). Not only has God graced him with continuing hunger so that he can keep eating with his stream of visitors, but his visitors, too, should join him in what we might call a "fast in reverse"—eating for hospitality's sake when one would rather not. In another instance, a monk apologizes for visiting a hermit and so breaking his rule. The hermit replies, "My rule is to welcome you with hospitality, and to send you on your way in peace" (XIII.7).

In dismissing "niceness" as a rationale for monastic hospitality, I do not mean to disparage the much thicker theological notion of "kindness." We have often commented on the extraordinary gentleness of the *Sayings*, in which even a meager effort at faithfulness is abundantly rewarded (e.g., XIII.6). Here, kindness is shown to be *evangelical*, as a heretical priest is won over by a monk who offers him hospitality without the accompanying lecture on doctrine that he had anticipated (XIII.11). Even more impressive, a priest is dressed down for shaming a begging widow when she took too much barley: "If you wanted to make her a gift, why were you so exact about the measure that you made her ashamed?" (XIII.14). Kindness, then, reflects God's way with his wayward creatures and ought also then to mark our interactions with others.

Even more, the desert fathers favored hospitality over fasting because it served as a spiritual version of hitting two birds with one stone: "A fast has its own reward, but whoever eats because of love, obeys two commandments: he loses his self-will, and he refreshes his brothers" (XIII.10). That is, the angst a fasting monk might feel at breaking his fast could itself be a spiritual aid, as it keeps him from pride and reminds him that obedience is more important than achievement. Another old hermit is made to eat out of schedule by a visitor. When others ask if this did not upset him, he answers, "I am upset when I do my own will" (XIII.8). Here, we see that indeed all things can work together for good to them that love God—indeed, even temptations to laxity in ascetic discipline (Rom 8:28).

In the final saying of this section, we hear something of an "echo" of a venerable biblical tradition (XIII.15 echoing Matt 14:13–21; Mark 6:32–44; Luke 9:10–17; John 6:1–15). For Jesus, five loaves and two fish were enough to feed a mighty crowd. In this saying, one hermit responds to famine by giving away what little bread he has. Another responds by guarding what little he has lest others get it. The former is shown to be right (The scant reserve of bread shows itself inexhaustible to the one who gives it away.), while the bread nervously hoarded runs out quickly. Those with ears to hear will remember the feeding miracles in the gospels. We see here what John Milbank[1] has described as an instance of "non-identical repetition" of a scriptural story. That is, the circumstances here are a bit different (with monks instead of disciples, a famine instead of a forgetful crowd without daypacks, a rebuke against a greedy monk instead of against faithless followers). Yet the differences heighten awareness of the similarity; both stories tell of a God whose resources are inexhaustible and who wishes us to deal with need out of an assumption of abundance rather than of scarcity. For this is a God who "is always doing wonders" (XIII.9).

1. Milbank uses this description in several places. See his "Can a Gift be Given? Prolegomena to a Future Trinitarian Metaphysic," in *Rethinking Metaphysics*, ed. L. G. Jones and Stephen Fowl (Oxford: Blackwell, 1995) 119–61.

Questions

1. The most difficult obstacle to hospitality to strangers in our day seems to be our fear of danger from them. Yet the desert itself was a dangerous place, and the monks' insistence on hospitality was nonetheless absolute. How does one negotiate this danger? Do poverty and chastity help?

2. The monks seem savvy to our concerns with panhandling—that money will be ill spent. How do they respond (XIII.12)?

3. Tell of an incident you know in which hospitality to strangers turned out to be a hosting of angels unawares. Do you have one in which it turned out to be a hosting of a less benign visitor?

XIV. Obedience

✣ A friend of mine spent a few weeks as a novice in a Benedictine monastery. I asked him why he left. Was it celibacy? "No," he said. "Sex is as often difficult as fulfilling; I could have done without." Was it poverty? "Are you kidding? Have you seen their building and library?" What then? "Obedience. Having to do what the guy who happens to be abbot says is hard enough when they're right. But when they're wrong, or they're not as talented as you, that was completely impossible." Counterintuitively perhaps, obedience is more difficult than poverty or chastity.

This section illustrates to us why. For obedience can easily be abused. In two sayings that echo the story of the (non)sacrifice of Isaac in Genesis 22, two monks are praised for their willingness to murder their sons. In both cases, the child does not die: the first because the abbot sent a counterorder that arrived at the last second; the second because of a miraculous cooling of a red-hot oven (XIV.8, 18). I cannot but think of those soldiers who have committed military atrocities, like Nazi prison guards or the murderers of civilians at My Lai, who responded that they were "merely following orders." Courts have rightly refuted such defenses, for surely no one should do something that is obviously morally reprehensible even if ordered. Here, monks are willing to sacrifice their children—a willingness that a Scripture-adherent people would have to allow is not outside the range of things God might order. (See Søren Kierkegaard for more on the "fear and trembling" that such passages rightly invoke.[1])

This section shows how differently the desert fathers evaluate obedience than we do. It is to be preferred even to chastity (XIV.9). A monk ought to heed his abbot's commands even more than the commands of God (XIV.12). It is the only thing that the newly converted need to know about (XIV.15). It is to be preferred to fasting, poverty, and even great charity! (XIV.7). As the final saying here says in praise of obedience, "It is the salvation of the faithful, the mother of all virtue, the entry into the kingdom; it raises us from earth to heaven; obedience lives in the same place as the angels; it is the food of the saints who by its nourishment grow to fullness of life" (XIV.19). Some of these sayings seem almost blasphemous in the amount of power and trust accorded to superiors.

Why such exuberant praise of obedience? Here, some demons tell us. When a desert ascetic follows the ever more demanding and even bizarre commands of his abbot, demons appear and complain that he is making them crazy: "If we praise you, you are quick to be humble; if we humble you, you rise up on high" (XIV.14). The final saying in this chapter gives a vision in which the obedient are rewarded more than those who suffer illness patiently, more than those who care for the sick, and more than hermits. "Those who care for others do what they themselves want to do. Hermits follow their own will in withdrawing from the world. But the obedient have gone beyond their self-will, and depend only on God and the word of their spiritual guides: that is why they shine the

---

1. Søren Kierkegaard, *Fear and Trembling; Dialectical Lyric by Johannes de silencio*, trans. Alastair Hannay, Penguin Classics (New York: Penguin, 1986).

most" (XIV.19). Obedience is a tonic for the kind of spiritual pride that so often accompanies great ascetic achievement. It is therefore necessary to every ascetic act and even to be preferred to those others. For someone who is proud only makes himself worse by adding spiritual achievement.

I read these sayings and think of the arguments I make when evangelical friends ask why to bother with the cold bureaucracy and stale piety of mainline denominations. Because, I have said, any authority is better than none. Echoing Roman Catholic arguments for having a pope or powerful bishops, I tend to say, "My submission even to a bishop whom I might dislike rightly mirrors Christian submission to God. In fact, it may do so better when I dislike the bishop!" Otherwise, one is always a lone ranger of a Christian, following what dictates one likes and excoriating those who differ.[2] With submission to an authority whom one may take to be mediocre, one's self-direction and sense of spiritual rightness must fade.[3]

Now, as dreary as that sounds, the *Sayings* speak of obedience in ways that approach uproarious humor. A calligrapher, when called by his superior, does not even finish the pen stroke on which he is working. His envious fellow novices learn then why he is so beloved, for "he had not finished the line of the O" (XIV.5). Or better still, John's master, Paul, tells him to pick up lion dung, and if approached by the lion, to tie her up and bring her. John does as he is told, chasing the

2. Rusty Reno makes this sort of argument in his *In the Ruins of the Church: Sustaining Faith in an Age of Diminished Christianity* (Grand Rapids: Eerdmans, 2002).

3. Let me hasten to add it has been nothing but a pleasure and inspiration to serve under Bishops Marion Edwards, Charlene Kammerer, Hee Soo-Jung, and Lawrence McClesky!

lion and shouting "Wait! My abba told me to tie you up!" The abbot cannot do other than act unimpressed, mercifully preserving John's humility: "Have you brought me that silly dog?" (XIV.14).

The miraculous potential of obedience remains, if not the humor, in a story about a monk planting a dead stick. After three years of the monk's constant watering, it turns green again and bears fruit. The hermit "picked some of the fruit and took it to church, and said to the brothers, 'Take and eat the fruit of obedience'" (XIV.3).[4] This does not happen. Dry twigs do not become a fertile fruit tree, except by virtue of a God who makes streams in the desert and a way in the wasteland. The small, precious nature of this miracle is underscored by the image of the monk passing around fruit in church. Obedience turns things green and bears sweet fruit.

Questions

1. Which is the greater danger: blind observance of demands for obedience, or proud forswearing of them?

2. Are the *Sayings* at their best when they are most "realistic," cognizant of human failures and less interested in the miraculous, or when they are most "fantastic," recounting things that do not ordinarily happen?

3. Is there a time when unpleasant obedience has made you more faithful?

---

4. Notice the echoes here to the parable in Luke 13:6–9. A friend who grew up on an apple farm assures me that if a fruit tree has not borne fruit for three years, it is, in fact, dead.

XV. Humility

Humility is not the first trait most observers would associate with Christians these days. Bitter divisions in our churches over hot-button moral issues and over how to relate faith to politics leave us in screaming matches with one another, in which we insist on our own holiness and right thinking and on the other's sinfulness and stupidity. For those on the outside looking in, it seems Christians are most intent on wanting to rule things, whether they are in favor of the conservatives now in power or of the liberals who wish they were.

In the fourth-century church, humility was no easier to attain than it is now, as these sayings make clear. In a more hierarchical society the opportunities for self-aggrandizement were rampant, especially since monks belonged to that small class of people who were literate, socially powerful, and eligible for positions of esteem or even worldly authority. The monks were not only "political" in that day, supporting or opposing the social policy of emperors based on whether they were sufficiently orthodox or not. They were also "celebrities," as the *Sayings* have already made clear, sought not only for advice but also so those seeking could brag to their friends back home. (Think of the guy waving with his cell phone in the crowd at sports events on television in our day.) This section's praise of humility should be heard against that background of those who sought desert anonymity becoming, perhaps paradoxically, all the more powerful and famous for it. We can see this in the saying about the emperor Theodosius visiting the monk outside Constantinople, thinking he is anonymous, though the monk knows who he is. When he reveals his identity, the hermit does obeisance, clearly not because he is surprised or impressed, but because humility suggests he ought. The emperor praises him, saying the humble bread and oil and salt is so good he has "never enjoyed bread and water as I have today" (XV.66). In response, the monk flees back to Egypt! In our age, when religious groups are desperate to have the emperor's ear (or to *be* emperor!), the hermit's horror at being praised, along with his dutifully serving his guest, seem extraordinary. His posture shows both the importance of humility to the desert fathers and the difficulty of pursuing it.

Perhaps it is too tepid to speak of the monks' "praise of humility." For they all but equate it with salvation itself. "I saw the devil's snares set all over the earth, and I groaned and said, 'What can pass through them?' I heard a voice saying, 'Humility'" (XV.3). Poemen said, "Humility is the ground on which the Lord ordered the sacrifice to be offered" (XV.37). He refers there to the Eucharist, which, in order to offer, the priest should stand on humility—no easy task when a priest was an important figure. The desert mother Syncletica says, "A ship cannot be built without nails and no one can be saved without humility" (XV.48). This is no small virtue required with ease.

Humility's most important feature seems to be silence. This is striking, especially since what seekers want from monks and hermits is "a word" that will aid their salvation. The great Antony, patron saint of all monastics as he is, is confused about "theodicy," as we moderns call it: the question of why bad things happen to good people. He is given no profound answer, but rather is told by God, "Antony, worry about yourself; these other matters are up to God, and it will not do you any good to know them" (XV.1). Quite a different answer than those of us would give who are inclined to write learned tomes about great mysteries. Antony also praises Brother Joseph for giving the best possible answer to a scriptural conundrum: "'What do you think is the meaning of this word?' He replies, 'I don't know.' Antony said, 'Indeed Joseph alone has found the true way, for he said he did not know'" (XV.4). Notice the actual question at hand is superfluous, not even worthy of mention! The point is to illustrate the posture to be taken toward Scripture and theology as such: one of not knowing. For a posture of professed wisdom or knowledge is a posture of pride, against which the saving way of humility sets itself. The great Archbishop Theophilus of Alexandria seeks a word from Abba Pambo, who is unwilling to give one other than this: "If he is not edified by my silence, my speech certainly will not edify him" (XV.42).

Silence is necessary for humility, but not sufficient. For the desert fathers, we also need recrimination. That is, active accusation and mistreatment by oneself and others. This is expressed most mildly in two sayings here that include characteristically dramatic gestures. In one, John describes the great Poemen's learning about humility from a certain abba named Anub. Anub throws rocks at a statue's face all day, and at the end of the day asks its forgiveness. He asks Poemen about the statue's reactions to the insults and the pardons, "When you saw me throwing stones at the statue's face, did it speak? Was it angry?" Its imperviousness both to mistreatment and to gentleness is the key to Christian community (XV.11). In another case, Zacharias responds violently to Moses's description of seeing the Holy Spirit descend upon him: he "took his cowl from his head, and put it beneath his feet and stamped on it, and said, 'Unless a man stamps upon himself like that, he cannot be a monk'" (XV.17).

These are the sorts of sayings we expect from the monks at this point—humility by way of self-recrimination. But what about when others accuse the desert fathers of wrongdoing? One hermit was asked why the monks were troubled by demons. He answered, "Because we throw away our armour, that is, humility, poverty, patience, *and men's scorn*" (XV.58, italics added). The first three are expected, but *scorn* as integral to monks' defense against demons? Abba Macarius gives an example of this with a story about the origin of his monastic vocation at Scetis: A local girl accused him of being the father of her unborn child. He did not deny it![1] The crowd mocked and abused and beat him publicly, and all the while he held his tongue. His response was to say to himself, "'Macarius, since you have found a wife for yourself, you need to work much harder to support her.' So I worked night and day and passed on to her the money that I made" (XV.25). The saying goes on to make his innocence clear, in supernatural and somewhat misogynist fashion. (Women were not only untrustworthy for ancient Christians but also sexually promiscuous by nature.) The interesting point for our purposes is that the *condition* of being accused and considered reprehensible by others was itself salutary for Macarius. He simply accepted the insults, statuelike, and took the woman's need for support to be part

1. Notice again the scriptural echoes: "Like a lamb silent before its shearer" (Acts 8:32 quoting Isa 53:7–8).

of his vocation to humility. For the desert fathers it is exceedingly important that one hold oneself to be guilty and one's opponents, such as there are, to be innocent. They can barely bring themselves to reproach another even when they are sure they are in the right, for that would break with humility born of silence (XV.76). A demon, before leaving his prey, asks his exorcising monk who the sheep and goats are. The monk responds, "The goats are people like myself; who the sheep are, God alone knows" (XV.65). Can anyone imagine our self-righteous, chest-thumping pundits today saying such a thing?

In this vein, it is noteworthy how often friction with demons appears in this section. Several times a demon tries to tempt a hermit by appearing as an angel or Christ himself, and each time the monk triumphs by claiming himself unworthy of a divine visitor. The humility sends the demon fleeing (XV.68, 70, 71). In one instance the devil himself explains this demonic tendency to the great Macarius: "I suffer a lot of violence from you, for I can't overcome you. For whatever you do, I do also. If you fast, I eat nothing; if you keep watch, I get no sleep. There is only one quality in which you surpass me . . . . Your humility; that is why I cannot prevail against you" (XV.26). The devil can do anything the saint can do, except give up his pride. This is not to say that it is easy to be done with pride and to shame the devils by humility. In one instance, humility is equated with love of enemies: "to do good to them that do evil to you" (XV.63). The demanding nature of this command, often reduced to saccharine sweetness when we discuss Jesus' insistence upon it, is shown in two rather offensive sayings about Moses submitting to racism and a slave submitting to his servitude (XV.29 & 31). In another case, humility is equated with accepting an apology *before it is offered*, which is another way of describing love of enemies (XV.63). A demon had his prey slap a monk on the cheek, the victim turned the other, and the demon cried, "Violence! The commandment of Jesus Christ is driving me out" (XV.14). Advocates of Christian nonviolence point out that while a willingness to go to war is prevalent in most of Christian history, a counterhistory of nonviolence is also present, in which those committed to monasticism would suffer violence rather than inflict it.[2]

The call to humility also put the monks in an awkward position with regard to church leadership. For surely these holy men could serve others, preferably as priests, or at least deacons? Yet the esteem afforded to such leaders would itself be a threat to the very humility that marked monastic life. (Remember the warning to flee from bishops!) One set of brothers does not flee, but humbly submits to ordination (XV.27). Yet nothing makes the monks actually preside at table, so they die without ever consecrating the elements! In another case Theodore is shown a pillar of fire stretching from earth to heaven when he asks God whether he should exercise his ministry (echoes of Gen 28:10–22 here). Who among us, if we saw such a sight, would not be impressed and consider it a sign to serve in the church? Theodore does the opposite. He

2. I owe this point to Hays, *The Moral Vision*: "The church's tradition also carries a significant and eloquent minority cloud of witnesses against violence . . . [who] have had a historic influence vastly disproportionate to their meager numbers, because their vision resonated so deeply with the New Testament and because their Christian witness therefore possessed such evident integrity" (341–42).

"determined never to exercise his ministry." When pressed, he swore, "If you do not let me alone, I will leave this place entirely" (XV.21). Not many should aspire to lead, or even to be close to God. If we do, we should do so prostrate, presuming nothing, on our faces (XV.57).

Questions

1. What dangers can you see to this call to humility? What dangers to ignoring it?

2. If the holiest among us were really the most humble, would the church have any leaders? How might one both lead and remain humble?

3. What demons have you seen overcome by nonviolence?

XVI. Patience

❧ When I think of patience, minor nuisances of late modern capitalism come to mind: waiting for a green light, unkind cashiers at big box chain department stores, crude gestures on freeways. When the desert fathers think of patience, they seem first to think of possessions, as in the recurring story in this section in which a monk either does nothing to stop, or actively helps, a thief stealing from his cell (XVI.1, 6, 19). They seem to think secondarily of long-suffering service to others, especially those who are abusive in some fashion (XVI.4, 18).

What exactly then is meant by the term *patience*? In scriptural parlance, it brings to mind the early church's waiting for Jesus' return and final bringing of the kingdom. The New Testament church clearly did extraordinary things in its belief that Jesus' return was imminent, such as swearing off sex and possessions. Monastics from every age are those who continue to do extraordinary things out of a similar belief, despite the long delay in that return. Given their trust in this soon-to-return Lord, thieves can be an aid, and mistreatment a positive help, in acquisition of patience. They can trust that God, and God alone, will right wrongs, so they can adopt a posture of waiting and hoping, rather than violently "fixing" what is wrong around them. This is illustrated profoundly in one of the funniest sayings of all, in which a brother offers a prayer on behalf of another who is insistent upon getting his revenge: "O God, we have no further need of you, for we can take vengeance by ourselves" (XVI.10).

Now in all these cases, the one whose harmful behavior is patiently borne is won over by the fathers' longsuffering: thieves repent, cruel abusers see the error of their ways, and monks are vindicated. In our world we rightly counsel people *not* to remain in abusive relationships, not to wait only on God for help, but to repair the situation or to remove themselves from it. Is there a way to arbitrate this dispute between their age of patient waiting for the eschaton and ours of refusing to be mistreated?

Theologian Sarah Coakley is a pioneer among feminist theologians in writing about the power of contemplative prayer.[1] Wordless prayer before God, she suggests, is not a submissive posture of misogyny but a liberating posture by which women can be filled with God's fullness and so live as abundantly as a creature can. This is because wordless prayer is an active taking part in the very inner triune "conversation" between the Father, the Son, and the Holy Spirit. When Romans 8 speaks of "groanings" that the Spirit prays in us when we have no words, Coakley hears her own experience of another praying in her as she prays. That other is the Spirit, praying to the Father. The one praying is part of that renewed creation that is slowly being returned to its creator in Christ. This dynamic of being caught up in the inner triune life is itself the most liberating posture possible for women, and it is one marked by silent patience. Other feminists, of course, may criticize Coakley's proposal. But is there space here for

1. This theme is present in several of the essays in Sarah Coakley, *Powers and Submissions: Spirituality, Philosophy, and Gender* (Oxford: Blackwell, 2002).

hearing these words from the desert fathers, words about silence in the midst of mistreatment, as liberative rather than problematic?

Questions

1. How would you define *patience* scripturally? (see 2 Pet 3:8 here).

2. How ought Christians to practice ownership in light of our expectation of Jesus' return (now, admittedly, delayed a little.)?

3. How do these sayings change the light in which you view your possessions? Or do they?

XVII. Charity

✣ The desert fathers would be disappointed if charity had not already appeared throughout the *Sayings* by this point. And indeed the themes of this section have already been sounded with some regularity. Yet, as it is for St. Paul, so it is for the desert fathers: the greatest of God's gifts is indeed love. So it is fitting to have a section dedicated specifically to it here toward the end of the collection (1 Cor 13:13). Further, this section suggests some ways that non-monks can approach an ascetic life. For if to be hung up by one's nose is not as great as love expressed in ministering to the sick, then there is hope for us who have not taken religious vows (and need for vigilance for those who have) (XVII.18).

"Hilarion once came from Palestine to Antony on the mountain. Antony said to him, 'Welcome, morning star, for you rise at break of day.' Hilarion said, 'Peace be to you, pillar of light, for you sustain the world'" (XVII.4). We can see here some nostalgic reminiscence of famous monks of the past, the sort of veneration of past practitioners necessary to pursue any craft, especially one so demanding as a disciplined Christian life. Yet can we not also see a glimpse of divine love—specifically in the extraordinarily exalted titles each of these famous monks gives to the other? "Morning star" is a favorite patristic description of Christ himself. "Pillar of light" recalls the very divine presence that led the Israelites in the wilderness. The simple greeting between the two monks suggests a high level of mutual regard, perhaps the sort of avuncular bonhomie we often share with fellow church members with a greeting on Sundays, whether we delve into deeper conversation with them or not. Yet the use of specifically *christological* descriptors suggests the monks' due regard for one another comes from seeing each other in the light of Christ. We might see not only holy monks in such exalted light, but all those for whom Christ died and was raised. So also in this section monks are given exalted degrees of love even when they get lost in the woods and endanger the whole group (XVII.7). They are loved well just because they are the opposing party in a dispute (XVII.6 & 8). They are loved well when they sin, and need help bearing a heavy penance (XVII.14). Perhaps most important, others are loved well when they are *still in unrepented sin*, for "if you do good to a good brother it is nothing to him, but to the other give double charity, for he is sick" (XVII.23).

The *Sayings* do more than reflect the christologically shaped love for sinners, important as that is. They also reflect a Holy-Spirit-infused love within the church among those who have been baptized, who have repented, and who seek now to live in community. For such people will be able to live among one another with grace and even without conflict. "Two hermits lived together for many years without a quarrel" (XVII.22). This is not a little impressive, as any married couple will tell you; often, living without a quarrel means one partner has long since succumbed to the other. But not here. For one hermit suggests, "'Let us have a quarrel with each other, as other men do.'" Perhaps here he has sinned, wanting to experience a conflict that is foreign to him. "'I don't know how a quarrel happens.' The first said, 'Look here, I put a brick between us, and I say, "That's mine." Then you say, "No, it's mine." That is how you begin a quarrel.'" Notice the message here: these two do not know what is "valuable," for they decide to quarrel over a brick, not wealth or food or prestige. Perhaps those things over which the rest of us quarrel are as little intrinsically valuable as this brick. "So they put a brick between them, and one of them said, 'That's mine.' The other said, 'No; it's mine.' He answered, 'Yes, it's yours. Take it away.' They were unable to argue with each other." These two are so practiced in regard for others, in selfless setting aside of their own wills, and in preference for harmony over division in community that they literally cannot fight when they want to.

This is the shape of specifically Christian charity or love. It begins for those who are enemies, in a quarrel, at odds with God and others. It offers self-sacrificial love in the presence of potential violence from the enemy (XVII.12). The compelling nature of the love offered brings about repentance and desire for new life in community. That community makes mutual regard and vigilance against slander of others its life, so as to be the community of love that first drew them to its midst. As God has loved us, so must we love one another.

112 AN INTRODUCTION TO THE DESERT FATHERS

Questions

1. The great Antony may sum up the *Sayings* as a whole in his description of loving God rather than fearing him (XVII.1). Is Antony's love greater specifically *because* he first passed through fear of God? That is, is someone who has wrestled with Christian asceticism out of some fear of God more equipped to say "God is love" than are we who have simply lived comfortably?

2. Do sayings such as XVII.22, with its description of monks who cannot fight, really help very much those of us who fight quite a lot? Or are they just discouraging?

XVIII. Visions

✣ We have already seen the desert fathers' concern about visions. They can easily be faked and used by demons to trick gullible monks. Why are they here praised?

First we should say that we can catch a glimpse of the history of the desert fathers as well as some of their polemical infighting. The monastic settlements in places like Scete were indeed attacked several times until the area was simply abandoned by Christian monastics. As all religious communities are wont to do, the desert fathers attribute their coming doom to their community's sins (XVIII.8, 11). We can also see a theological debate that sounds disarmingly familiar, since its terms have been fought over again multiple times in the church's history. Is the Eucharist the actual body and blood of Christ or a symbol of some sort (XVIII.3)?

Historical questions aside, we can ask the theological question of why the visions recounted here should be trusted while those disparaged elsewhere in the *Sayings* should not be? A tentative answer is that these visions offer the monks and their communities glimpses of *the way things are.*[1] That is, monks are not shown visions as religious fireworks meant to impress them or their friends, or to grant more prestige to be bartered around the monastery. Rather, here what we normally take to be reality is peeled back for a moment, and a more basic reality is shown to be, just below its surface. In

1. This is Stanley Hauerwas's claim about the nature of theology generally—that it describes "the grain of the universe"—in his *With the Grain of the Universe: The Church's Witness and Natural Theology* (Grand Rapids: Brazos, 2001).

reality, legions of angels stand and fight on behalf of humbly penitent friends of prayer, and hoards of demons stand on the side of proud sowers of dissension (XVIII.12). In reality, crowns come to rest on the heads of those who die for the faith (XVIII.14). In reality, a despised woman, taken by her companions to be a pitiable maniac worthy only of abuse, is a holy woman, a saint, an "amma" (XVIII.19). It is the profoundest of realities that the Word of God shapes hearts as water does a rock—slowly, almost indiscernibly, but certainly, so that after years one can look back and see its work (XVIII.16).

Questions

1. What is the effect of these miraculous vision sayings? Do they evoke awe or mirth?

2. How does one tell a miraculous vision from a deceitful ploy of a demon?

3. What intersection is there between these sorts of celestial sightings and the ordinary lives of those of us who see no such thing?

4. Philip Rousseau speaks of the *Sayings* this way: "Each entry . . . in this fascinating series captures the attention of the reader like a flash of a signaling lamp—brief, arresting, and intense."[2] What have you learned from the *Sayings* in general? Especially, what have you learned from the desert fathers' manner of writing theology—a manner shocking, appealing, converting?

---

2. Quoted in Harmless, *Desert Christians*, 169.

Bibliography

(This list is not meant to be exhaustive, by any means. But this is a start; following the footnotes in these texts will lead you to further and more detailed resources.)

Athanasius. *The Life of Antony.* Translated by Robert Gregg. Classics of Western Spirituality. New York: Paulist, 1980.

Antony was the standard-bearer for many of the ancient desert fathers, and this description of his own life sparked similar spiritual imaginations for countless imitators.

Benedict, Saint, Abbot of Mote Cassino. *The Rule of St. Benedict*, translated by Anthony C. Meisel and M. L. del Maestro. An Image book original. New York: Image, 1975.

Benedict's extensive instructions for how to live as a cloistered, monastic community is interesting both for its similarities to and its differences from the Sayings *material.*

Bianco, Frank. *Voices of Silence: Lives of the Trappists Today.* New York: Paragon House, 1991.

In this portrait, several living, breathing, Trappist monks become full-blooded people rather than the cartoons to which we're tempted to reduce them.

Brown, Peter. *The Body and Society: Men, Women, and Sexual Renunciation in Early Christianity.* New York: Columbia University Press, 1988.

The standard account of Christian ascetic practice in the early church is also wonderfully engaging. If the move to give up sex and live in the desert seems ridiculous to you, Brown explains the motives of those who did so with unsurpassed skill.

Burton-Christie, Douglas. *The Word in the Desert: Scripture and the Quest for Holiness in Early Christian Monasticism.* New York: Oxford University Press, 1993.

What was originally Burton-Christie's dissertation at the University of Virginia challenged the stock Protestant dismissal of monastic readings of

Scripture and argues that the Sayings display a subtle and complex biblical hermeneutic. More engaging reading, by far, than most dissertations.

Chryssavgis, John. *In the Heart of the Desert: The Spirituality of the Desert Fathers and Mothers, with a Translation of Father Zosimas' Reflections.* Treasures of the World's Religions. Bloomington, IN: World Wisdom, 2003.

Another scholarly, readable, and beautiful account of the desert tradition, which includes photographs of some of the desert locations in which the monks lived as well as icons of some of the most beloved practitioners of desert monasticism.

Downey, Michael, and Michael Mauney. *Trappist: Living in the Land of Desire.* New York: Paulist: 1997.

A truly stunning book of photographs and essays from life at Mepkin Abbey in Moncks Corner, South Carolina.

Harmless, William. *Desert Christians: An Introduction to the Literature of Early Monasticism.* Oxford: Oxford University Press, 2004.

Harmless's book is a crucial resource for the church's desert literature. Not only more accessible than previous accounts, which tended to be aimed more at scholars, it also includes translations of key monastic texts that are difficult to find elsewhere—a model for how to write in a way that helps both general readers and experts.

Louth, William. *The Wilderness of God.* London: Darton, Longman and Todd, 1991.

An exploration of the place of the desert in Christians' worldview, from the Scriptures to the twentieth century. Especially helpful for its comparisons between the desert fathers and figures about whom English-reading Protestants will likely know nothing, such as Charles de Foucauld and Père Surin.

Merton, Thomas, trans. *The Wisdom of the Desert: Sayings from the Desert Fathers of the Fourth Century.* New York: New Directions, 1960.

One of the monastic life's most important twentieth-century popularizers here gives his own brief introduction to their literature and his own translations of what he takes to be the most important of the Sayings.

The Monks of New Skete. *In the Spirit of Happiness: Spiritual Wisdom for Living.* Boston: Little, Brown, 1999.

A monastery of Eastern Orthodox monks best known for a wonderful guide on how to raise your dog, here dispense hearty portions of spiritual wisdom.

Ward, Benedicta, translator. *The Desert Fathers: Sayings of the Early Christian Monks.* Penguin Classics. New York: Penguin, 2003.

A vivid and engaging translation of this classic text.

————. *The Harlots of the Desert: A Study of Repentance in Early Monastic Sources.* Cistercian Studies Series 106. Kalamazoo, MI: Cistercian, 1987.

The standard account of the Sayings' *depiction of the desert mothers.*

————, translator. *The Sayings of the Desert Fathers: An Alphabetical Collection.* Kalamazoo, MI: Cistercian, 1975.

Ancient preservers of the desert tradition recorded the Sayings *in two ways, one as we have studied here in the Penguin edition, the other in an alphabetical listing according to the monks' names. This volume is a handy way to study all the* Sayings *about, say, Macarius as opposed to in the theme-based arrangement we attend to here.*

Williams, Rowan. "Acrobats and Jugglers." In *The Wound of Knowledge: A Theological History from the New Testament to Luther and St. John of the Cross*, 90–115. Eugene, OR: Wipf and Stock, 1998.

Technical but still quite accessible description of desert spirituality within the larger story Williams tells about the history of spirituality in the church.

————. *Where God Happens: Discovering Christ in One Another.* Boston: New Seeds, 2005.

Williams's lectures to a community of monastics and committed lay people in Australia, complete with the transcript of an exciting question-and-answer session between Williams and his audience.